English Language Learners:

Differentiating Between Language Acquisition and Learning Disabilities

Janette Klingner and Amy M. Eppolito

Council for
Exceptional
Children
The voice and vision of special education

Council for Exceptional Children
2900 Crystal Drive, Suite 1000
Arlington, VA 22202-3557
www.cec.sped.org

Parts of Chapter 2 and Chapter 6 are adapted with permission from *Why Do English Language Learners Struggle With Reading? Distinguishing Language Acquisition From Learning Disabilities,* by J. K. Klingner, J. Hoover, and L. Baca. Copyright 2008 by Corwin Press.

Printed in the United States of America

Library of Congress Cataloging-in-Publication data

Klingner, Janette.
    English language learners: Differentiating between language acquisition and learning
    disabilities / by Janette Klingner and Amy M. Eppolito.
    p. cm.
    Includes biographical references.

ISBN 978-0-86586-478-8

Stock No. P6120

Cover and interior design by Tom Karabatakis

First edition

10 9 8 7 6 5

Table of Contents

Introduction 1

Chapter 1   Who Are ELLs? How Can We Determine if an ELL's Struggles
With Reading in English Are Due to LD or Language Acquisition? 7

Chapter 2   What Are Some of the Characteristics of Language Acquisition
That Can Mirror LD? 13

Chapter 3   What Are Some of the Different Types of ELLs and
Why Are These Distinctions Important? 23

Chapter 4   What Does It Mean to Consider "Opportunity to Learn"
When Determining Whether Students May Have LD? .31

Chapter 5   What Are Some Common Misconceptions About ELLs and the
Second Language Acquisition Process? What Are the Realities? 47

Chapter 6   In What Ways Is Learning to Read in English as a Second or
Additional Language Different Than Learning to Read in English
as a First Language That Can Be Confusing for ELLs? 61

Chapter 7   How Can Schools Establish Structures to Facilitate the Process for
Distinguishing Between Language Acquisition and Learning Disabilities? 69

Chapter 8   How Are Families Involved in the Process? 79

Chapter 9   How Can We Tell Which ELLs Should Be Referred for a
Comprehensive Evaluation? 91

Chapter 10   What Does It Mean to Use an Ecological Framework to
Determine Whether ELLs Have LD? 99

References 105

Introduction

Whether you are a special education teacher, a general education teacher, a psychologist, a social worker, a parent, an administrator, or someone else in a support role, these are exciting times to be working with English language learners (ELLs)[1]. In a recent article in the *The New York Times,* Bhattacharjee (2012) pointed out the cognitive benefits of bilingualism, noting that being bilingual can "make you smarter," and that bilingualism can have a "profound effect on your brain, improving cognitive skills not related to language and even shielding against dementia in old age" (p. SR12). Bhattacharjee explained that, until recently, many experts believed that the challenges faced by bilinguals when figuring out which of their languages to use caused interference or confusion. However, as Martin-Rhee and Bialystok (2008) research showed, whenever bilingual individuals speak, both (or all) of their languages are active. Rather than causing interference, the challenge of figuring out how best to communicate provides a "cognitive workout" that can actually strengthen the brain. Bilinguals are generally believed to be more flexible thinkers and better than monolinguals at solving certain kinds of mental puzzles. They may be able to out-perform their monolingual peers because of enhanced executive functioning (i.e., the brain's ability to plan, monitor understanding, apply strategies, ignore distractions, and solve problems).

Why is this important? It is significant for bilingual individuals as well as for everyone else. In its *Blueprint for Reform* (U.S. Department of Education, 2010), the Obama Administration stated that an important goal for the United States as a nation is to produce high school graduates who are fully bilingual and multicultural and ready to compete in the global economy. If that is the case, then we should regard students who begin school already knowing another language besides English as having a head start over their peers. If we nurture their bilingualism and capitalize on their linguistic, cultural, and experiential strengths—helping them to feel "smart" rather than "at risk" —then we will enrich their school experiences as well as our own (Klingner, Vaughn, & Boardman, in press). We can do this by making sure ELLs have every opportunity to interact with peers and use academic language, engage in higher level thinking, and contribute in their classrooms and schools in meaningful ways. As delineated by the CEC position statement on instruction for ELLs with learning disabilities (LD; see box, Essential Components), everyone who works with ELLs should learn how best to support their language acquisition as well as their academic and social development.

---

[1] We use the terms *English language learner* and *emerging bilingual student* to refer to those students in the process of acquiring English who are not yet fully proficient.

Essential Components of Special Education for English Language Learners With Learning Disabilities

A seamless, supportive education for English language learners (ELLs) with learning disabilities (LD) includes many essential components. When ELLs are identified as having LD, their need for instruction in English language development does not end (Gersten & Baker, 2000; Rodriguez, Carrasquillo, & Lee, 2014; Zehler et al., 2003), nor do the benefits of instruction in their home language cease. In other words, ELLs with LD need the services designed to support both students with LD and ELLs. These learners benefit from (a) culturally and linguistically responsive teachers; (b) culturally and linguistically responsive and relevant instruction; (c) a supportive learning environment; (d) assistance with English language acquisition (such as oral language, vocabulary, and academic language development) and support with the home language; (e) help in the general education classroom with accessing the general education curriculum; and (f) intensive research-based interventions designed to help improve academic and, possibly, behavioral skills in targeted areas.

Culturally and Linguistically Responsive Teachers

Whether in the general or special education classroom, teachers who are responsive to their students' cultural and linguistic needs share many features (Huerta, 2011; Kea & Trent, 2013; Ladson-Billings, 2001; Lucas, Villegas, & Freedson-Gonzalex, 2008; Nieto, 2003). These teachers build strong relationships with students and their families. They hold high expectations and know how to scaffold instruction to help students meet those expectations. They do not give up. When a student does not succeed, rather than conclude the student cannot be successful, they try a different approach. They connect learning with students' experiences and interests, making learning relevant to students' lives, and they value and build on different ways of knowing. These responsive teachers also help students to develop a critical consciousness so that they can be aware of and challenge society's inequities (Kea & Trent, 2013; Ladson-Billings, 1995).

Linguistically responsive teachers understand the second language acquisition process and know how to support ELLs' growth in language and literacy (Rodriguez, Carrasquillo, & Lee, 2014) . They view bilingualism as an asset. They understand how learning to read in a second or additional language is similar to and different from learning to read in a first language, how to differentiate instruction to meet diverse students' needs, how culture affects learning, and how to use assessment procedures that are sensitive to cultural differences and provide an accurate portrayal of students' strengths as well as their learning needs (Ortiz, & Artiles, 2010; Teachers of English to Speakers of Other Languages, 2008).

Culturally and Linguistically Responsive and Relevant Instruction

Culturally responsive instruction (Gay, 2002; Kea & Trent, 2013; Ladson-Billings, 2001) emphasizes relevance to students' lives and builds on their prior knowledge, interests, and motivation. It includes the explicit teaching of school-expected norms for participation while validating the interactional and communicative styles that students have learned in their homes and communities (Rodriguez, Ringler, O'Neal, & Bunn, 2009). It creates literacy activities that build on and expand students' home literacy experiences such as storytelling, writing autobiographies and personal narratives, or writing letters to family members. It incorporates students' and their families' knowledge and expertise into instruction (Moll, Amanti, Neff, & Gonzalez, 1992; Murry, 2012).

Linguistically responsive instruction (Lucas, Villegas, & Freedson-Gonazalez, 2008) is understandable (i.e., comprehensible) for ELLs and appropriate for their language proficiency levels. It includes language objectives and language supports and develops linguistic competence through purposeful classroom dialogue and frequent opportunities to learn and use academic language. It includes explicit attention to linguistic forms and functions.

A Supportive Learning Environment

A supportive environment facilitates learning and promotes positive school experiences. Students feel safe and are comfortable taking risks. They need not fear that their efforts at communication will be thwarted. Students frequently collaborate with one another in mutually beneficial ways. They can be active learners and feel competent and successful. It is important to keep in mind that ELLs with LD can appear to be competent in one context but not another (Harry & Klingner, 2006) and can seem very different across dissimilar educational settings (López-Reyna, 1996). Therefore, it is imperative to examine all learning environments to make sure that students are thriving and are receiving the support they need (Herrera, Perez, Escamilla, 2010).

Assistance With English Language Acquisition

Regardless of the setting, ELLs require explicit instruction that supports their oral language, vocabulary, and academic language development (August & Shanahan, 2006; Francis, Rivera, Lesaux, Kieffer, & Rivera, 2006; Genesee, Lindholm-Leary, Saunders, & Christian, 2006; Gersten, & Baker 2000; Goldenberg, 2008; Snow, Lawrence, & White, 2009). Teachers must create learning situations where students can interact with peers in meaningful ways. Effective vocabulary instruction for ELLs must be frequent, intensive, systematic, and complex and should include strategy instruction that helps students learn words independently (Klingner, 2012).

Support in General Education Classrooms

Like other students with LD, ELLs with LD are entitled to support that helps them access the general education curriculum (Genesee, Lindholm-Leary, Saunders, & Christian, 2006). These supports include modifications and adaptations recommended for ELLs (e.g., Sheltered English techniques) as well as accommodations for students with disabilities. Garcia and Tyler (2010) suggest that teachers first identify common barriers to learning for their ELLs with LD, and then implement strategies that have been shown to be effective with similar students. Possibilities include providing extra time to complete tasks, clarifying complex directions, providing visual supports, recording reading assignments for homework or review, providing peer tutoring, and breaking longer presentations into shorter segments.

Intensive Research-Based Interventions

Last but certainly not least, ELLs with LD must receive intensive research-based interventions designed to help them improve their academic and, as needed, their behavioral skills in targeted areas. Some consider these individualized, intensive interventions to be the "hallmark" of special education (Vaughn, Denton, & Fletcher, 2010). For ELLs, the language of intervention should match the language of classroom reading instruction (Ortiz, 2001). Interventions should be designed specifically for and validated with ELLs who struggle with reading. In other words, interventions that have only been shown to be effective for monolingual speakers are inadequate. Vaughn and colleagues (e.g., Vaughn, Cirino et al., 2006; Vaughn, Mathes, Linan-Thompson, & Francis, 2005; Vaughn, Mathes et al., 2006) included the following elements in their interventions for ELLs:

- Explicit instruction in oral language and listening comprehension
- Explicit instruction in reading comprehension strategies
- A read-aloud routine with explicit vocabulary instruction and scaffolded story retelling
- Word study and phonics strategies
- Word reading and reading connected texts
- Repeated reading for speed, accuracy, fluency, and prosody

Conclusion

Providing special education for ELLs with LD will require collaboration among the various teachers and support personnel in a school. For example, special education teachers unfamiliar with the process of second language acquisition and sheltering techniques should partner with English as a Second Language (ESL) teachers and/or Teachers of English to Speakers of Other Languages (TESOL)-endorsed content teachers. Similarly, ESL teachers can seek advice from their special education colleagues. Together, we share more expertise than any one of us alone.

Note. Reprinted with permission from Essential Components of Special Education for English Language Learners With Learning Disabilities. Position Statement of the Division for Learning Disabilities of the Council for Exceptional Children, by J. Klingner, A. Boelé, S. Linan-Thompson, & D. Rodriguez. Copyright 2014 Council for Exceptional Children Division for Learning Disabilities.

About This Book

English Language Learners addresses some common questions and confusion about ELLs and learning disabilities (LD) that have come up in our conversations with our colleagues in the education field. In the first chapter, we explain who ELLs are and how educators can determine if an ELL's struggles with reading in English are due to LD or language acquisition. Chapter 2 addresses some of the characteristics of language acquisition that can mirror LD. Then, in the third chapter, we provide additional information about some of the different types of ELLs and why these distinctions are important. We follow with an explanation in Chapter 4 of what it means to consider "opportunity to learn" when evaluating whether students may have LD. In the fifth chapter, we contrast some misconceptions and realities about ELLs and the second language acquisition process. Chapter 6 highlights ways that learning to read in English as a second or additional language is different than learning to read in English as a first language, and how that can be confusing for ELLs. In the seventh and eighth chapters, we describe how schools can establish structures to facilitate the process for distinguishing between language acquisition and learning disabilities and family involvement in the process. Chapter 9 suggests guidelines for determining how which ELLs should be referred for a comprehensive evaluation. Finally, in the last chapter, we discuss what it means to use an ecological framework to determine whether ELLs have LD.

CHAPTER 1

Who Are ELLs? How Can We Determine if an ELL's Struggles With Reading in English Are Due to LD or Language Acquisition?

This chapter addresses:
- Demographics of ELLs
- Prevalence of ELLs with learning disabilities
- Challenges of identifying ELLs with learning disabilities
- Distinguishing language acquisition and learning disabilities

The United States is becoming increasingly diverse. Perhaps you now have ELLs in your class or classes but in previous years you did not. It used to be that ELLs concentrated in certain states and pockets in the United States—but now they can be anywhere. ELLs are the fastest growing section of the student population. Recently, over a 10-year period, the increase in ELLs nationwide was about 51%, whereas the total preK–12 student population only increased by about 7.22% (National Clearinghouse for English Language Acquisition, 2011). The vast majority of ELLs speak Spanish as their first language, although many other first languages are also represented (Aud et al., 2011). Latinos/Hispanics totaled about 16.5% of the U.S. population in 2009 and included about 50 million people (Fry & Lopez, 2012; Hemphill & Vanneman, 2011). Across the United States, in 2011, about 25% of the public elementary school population and about 21% of the high school population was Hispanic (Fry & Lopez, 2012). In addition, states such as California (Kane, 2010) and Texas (Smith, 2012) have a majority of Hispanic students in their public schools.

ELLs tend to underachieve in comparison with fluent English-speaking classmates on tests of English literacy (e.g., Abedi, 2002). Data from the 2009 National Assessment of Educational Progress (NAEP) show a 25-point gap between Whites and Hispanics in fourth-grade reading achievement and a 24-point discrepancy at eighth grade (Hemphill & Vanneman, 2011). Other issues correlate with these scores, such as whether or not the students receive free or reduced-price lunch. In any case, it is clear that we must help improve ELLs' reading comprehension.

However, many teachers and support personnel are not adequately prepared to meet their ELLs' literacy and language needs (Zehler et al., 2003). Teachers described feeling "challenged to help these children reach the level of proficiency required for learning sophisticated academic content through English" (Dixon et al., 2012, p. 6). Now that the Common Core State Standards (see www.corestandards.org for more information) are here with their emphasis on increasingly complex texts, these challenges can seem even more overwhelming.

ELLs With LD

About 7.6% of the ELLs in the United States are believed to have a disability (National Center for Education Statistics, 2009; Peña, Bedore, & Gillam, 2011). Percentages vary a lot by state, however, from highs of 28.36% in California, 20.50% in New Mexico, 16.70% in Nevada, and 15.45% in Texas to a low of 0.35% in Virginia. Identification rates also vary within and across districts (Artiles, Rueda, Salazar, & Higareda, 2005; Sullivan, 2011). The majority (about 55%) of those ELLs identified with a disability are thought to have LD (Peña et al., 2011). Yet determining whether an ELL actually has LD can be quite difficult; the multidisciplinary team must be able to establish that the ELL's learning difficulties are not primarily the result of language acquisition (Individuals With Disabilities Education Improvement Act, IDEA, 2006). To do so, the team need not wait until the student is fully proficient in English. Instead, it means that they must ascertain that ELLs exhibit the characteristics of both LD and language acquisition. In other words, students should be struggling in their first language as well as in English.

The team also must determine that the student has received an adequate opportunity to learn through research-based instructional and intervention practices that have been validated with other ELLs (see Chapter 4), although it can be difficult to make judgment calls such as these (Klingner, Artiles, & Méndez Barletta, 2006). One way is to look at class data sets to see how ELLs in general are doing in comparison to "true" peers (i.e., same-language, same-age peers with similar background experiences).

ELLs with LD are usually taught by special educators who have received inadequate preparation in how to meet ELLs' language and literacy needs (Barker & Grassi, 2011). In fact, when they are placed into special education, many ELLs lose access to specialized language instruction, such as through English Language Development (ELD), English as a Second Language (ESL), or Structured English Immersion (SEI) programs (Zehler et al., 2003). There seems to be a mistaken belief that special education and ESL services should be thought of as "either/or"—that once ELLs qualify for special education, they no longer qualify for language support services. An important principle to keep in mind is that ELLs with LD are entitled to a full range of seamless services designed to meet their individual language and learning needs.

Throughout this book we use ELL, emerging bilingual (EB), and culturally and linguistically diverse (CLD) interchangeably. We steer away from using the term *limited English proficient* (LEP), although this terminology is pervasive throughout policy and practice. Categorizing children LEP generates predominantly negative connotations: It focuses on what they cannot do—yet—rather than on their numerous strengths. The term LEP dates from the Elementary and Secondary Education Act of 1965 and continues to be used for legislative purposes to this day. Although the term serves to identify ELLs who are in need of educational assistance based on their linguistic status and to appropriate funding for such programs, it also sets up a "limited" mindset towards ELLs. Concerns about the negativity of the LEP label have been voiced recently and consistently by those in the educational community (Crawford, 2004; MacSwan 2000; Ovando, Collier, & Combs, 2003). In sum, labels such as ELL, EB, and CLD are meant and perceived to be more positive.

Distinguishing Between Language Acquisition and LD

To be able to distinguish language acquisition from LD, educators must understand the second language acquisition process, recognize characteristics associated with LD, and be able to assess the quality of instruction in students' classrooms. Have these students truly received an adequate opportunity to learn?

Struggles with English language acquisition, on the surface, can seem to mirror characteristics of LD. Digging deeper and trying to understand the reasons for certain behaviors is essential to identifying the underlying causes. We recommend using a hypothesis-driven approach to determining whether an ELL has LD. Begin the referral and evaluation process by exploring the hypothesis that the causes of the student's learning difficulties are primarily external factors (rather than internal to the child). Conduct the assessment with the notion that there is nothing wrong with the individual and that systemic, ecological, or environmental factors are the primary reason for learning problems. Maintain this hypothesis until data suggest otherwise and all plausible external factors have been ruled out. The point is not to look for whom or what to blame for a child's struggles, but rather to understand the multiple complex factors that are affecting the child's learning and performance.

There are many reasons why an ELL may not respond to a particular instructional approach in the way we intend (Klingner & Edwards, 2006). It is possible that the instruction or intervention is not as effective for this child as for others, and a different method would yield better results. It could be that the student needs more language support, or that the level of instruction is not a good match for the child. Another possibility is that the environment is not conducive to learning. Before referring a student for an evaluation, consider the classroom environment, observe instruction, and recommend different approaches.

Classroom example: Michele teaches first grade at Garvey Elementary School. She has been teaching there for 14 years and has seen the community change from almost all White middle class families to mostly Latino working class families who work at the new plant nearby. More than half of Michele's students speak Spanish in their homes, and about 36% are in the process of acquiring English—or, in other words, are ELLs.

Michele has a Master's degree in Elementary Education and her principal considers her to be an effective teacher, although she personally feels that she has "the wrong master's" for the school's changing demographics. Because the school district selected Garvey Elementary to be a pilot response-to-intervention (RTI) school, Michele recently attended district-sponsored professional development workshops on progress monitoring and other components of RTI. Like many schools around the country, her district is pushing the use of evidence-based practices as "what works."

Yet, Michele has not taken any coursework or received any professional development in teaching ELLs how to read. She does not know about second language acquisition or understand much about LD. She supposes that the evidence-based reading practices touted on the What Works Clearinghouse web site are appropriate for all students. She ponders, "Isn't good teaching just good teaching?"

The problem with thinking this way is that the answer to that question is a resounding "No!" If your belief is that you can teach your ELLs in the same way, with the same materials you have been using in the past with students from different demographics, then you are bound to experience some challenges. Michele's students are struggling, and she is not sure why. Like so many other teachers who are ill prepared to work with ELLs, she assumes that the problems reside in her students and their families, and perhaps the community. She thinks that one reason her current students are not faring well is that they started school underprepared. For example, she compares them with her previous students on prereading aspects such as knowing letter names and sounds and realizes that fewer students started school with this knowledge. Yet she has not changed her curriculum. In other words, she expects the students to adjust rather than her instruction. She believes that aspects related to living below the nation's poverty line create additional challenges for them. She thinks of not being fully proficient in English as setting up barriers, and she feels very discouraged that, despite what she thinks of as her best efforts to meet their needs, many of her ELLs are still not learning to read. She wonders whether a disproportionate number of them might have LD.

It is common for teachers to misunderstand ELLs' lack of progress and blame it on the students (Orosco & Klingner, 2010). Being an effective teacher with one demographic group is not the same as being an effective teacher with all students. A typical scenario is that a principal or a language arts director in the school district advises using a specific instructional or intervention approach, stressing that it is research based. The principal might even emphasize that the method has been "proven" to work. When this happens, teachers assume that, because they are using an evidence-based practice, when their ELLs do not progress, it must be because the students are somehow deficient. Yet students do not all learn in the same way. What works with some students is not the same as asking what works with whom, in what settings, under what conditions, with which outcomes, and when taught by whom. Most commercially produced curricula in the United States have been developed based on assumptions about the "majority" White middle-class student in the United States and the cultural and linguistic knowledge of this demographic of student. ELLs differ from their mainstream peers in significant ways that can influence how successful instruction or an intervention will be (August & Shanahan, 2006; Goldenberg, 2008).

Conclusion

The vast majority of referrals for an evaluation for possible special education placement are made by classroom teachers (Ysseldyke, 2005). If teachers can improve their understanding of the reasons for ELLs' struggles, they will be less likely to judge them as lacking.

However, some ELLs truly do have LD and would benefit from the extra support they would receive in special education. Teachers should not wait until ELLs are fully proficient in English before deliberating whether they might have LD. The temptation is strong to delay concentrating on the possibility that ELLs are struggling with reading due to language acquisition or learning disabilities (Francis et al., 2006). It is understandable that, because the characteristics common to language acquisition can appear to mirror those of LD, school personnel may have a habit of waiting, to avoid the possibility of incorrectly placing an ELL in special education. Wanting to wait could actually be a sign that school personnel have some knowledge about the confusing aspects of language acquisition and LD. Just as it is a predicament to identify ELLs as having a disability when they do not, it is also a problem to delay providing interventions to ELLs who really need them. Following the guidelines outlined in this book can help improve instruction for all ELLs and result in fewer inappropriate referrals. The few ELLs who are still experiencing difficulties at that point will benefit from explicit, intensive interventions in addition to the instruction they are receiving in their general education classrooms.

Focus Questions

- What do you think is the most challenging aspect of distinguishing between language acquisition and LD?

- As a rule, do some of your subgroups of students do better than others? In other words, how do your ELLs do in comparison with other students?

CHAPTER 2

What Are Some of the Characteristics of Language Acquisition That Can Mirror LD?

This chapter addresses:
- Characteristics of LD that can mirror language acquisition
- Characteristics of language acquisition that can mirror LD
- How these characteristics are manifested when reading

For educators to be able to distinguish between characteristics associated with LD and characteristics of students struggling to acquire English as a second or additional language, they must be aware of the finer points of each of these challenges. As discussed in Chapter 1, instruction that "works" for their mainstream peers might not be as effective for ELLs (August & Shanahan, 2006; Goldenberg, 2008). This does not mean, however, that the student has a learning disability.

Learning Disabilities

Definition

The federal government has defined a *specific learning disability* as

> a disorder in 1 or more of the basic psychological processes involved in understanding or in using language, spoken or written, which disorder may manifest itself in the imperfect ability to listen, think, speak, read, write, spell, or do mathematical calculations. Such term includes such conditions as perceptual disabilities, brain injury, minimal brain dysfunction, dyslexia, and developmental aphasia. Such term does not include a learning problem that is primarily the result of visual, hearing, or motor disabilities, of intellectual disabilities, of emotional disturbance, or of environmental, cultural, or economic disadvantage. (20 U.S.C. §1401 [30][A]–[C])

The wording of the federal government definition is conceptual in nature and does not specify recognizable characteristics or definitive criteria for identification. Because of this lack of specificity, over the years many experts inside and outside of education have decried the definition's ambiguity and variability in interpretation. The term *basic psychological processes* is not defined in the federal regulations, for example, and the majority of states do not include this in their definitions. Professional groups (e.g., National Joint Committee on Learning Disabilities; Interagency Committee on Learning Disabilities) have attempted to resolve the issue by proposing alternative definitions, but none have successfully eliminated the vagueness or found a way to include widely accepted, specific criteria. Thus, to date, Congress has not adopted an alternative definition.

However, states are required by law to establish a means of identifying students who have learning disabilities. Since the 2004 reauthorization of IDEA, this has also meant that states may not require the use of a "severe discrepancy" model in this process, and must allow districts to use research-based interventions and evaluation procedures. (This latter language has resulted in an increase in states' incorporation of strategies such as response to intervention, RTI.) Every general education teacher should be knowledgeable of their district's policy and school procedures for identifying students with LD.

Characteristics

Students with LD are a heterogeneous group. Although there are certain characteristics that are commonly associated with LD, a student with LD may actually have only a few of the typical characteristics. The primary defining characteristic common to all students with LD is considerable academic difficulty in at least one area of academic functioning. This is the *outcome* of the underlying LD. Students with LD may struggle in one or more areas, such as literacy (including writing and oral language) and mathematics. Challenges with literacy are the most common form of LD. Other disabilities can co-occur with LD (as long as they are not the primary disabling condition) and may add to learning problems; examples include attention deficit hyperactivity disorder, conduct disorder, medical conditions, physical challenges, or emotional difficulties.

It can be easy to forget that each student with LD also is likely to have areas of strength. For example, fourth-grader Andrew has severe difficulties with reading and writing and this challenge pervades all his academic work. Yet, he also has strong points. His teachers recognize that he is improving in mathematics. Andrew is also sensitive, caring, and quite perceptive of others' feelings. He fits well socially into Mrs. Spencer's class and does not seem to exhibit any serious behavior problems. In fact, Mrs. Spencer thinks of him as a model student in terms of his determination and effort. She often gives him classroom responsibilities because he is so dependable. Andrew is her "right hand" with the computer stations in her room. He is very good at troubleshooting when students run into problems on the computer.

Second Language Acquisition

Now that we have explored the characteristics of learning disabilities, consider what is involved in the process of language acquisition (see Table 2.1). *Second language acquisition* is probably the term most frequently used to refer to the process of learning a new language—"second," even though the language might be the third, fourth, or fifth language the person is acquiring. Although linguists do not agree precisely on a second language acquisition process, it is generally accepted that ELLs pass through different stages on their way to proficiency. These five stages include some version of preproduction, early production, speech emergence, intermediate fluency, and advanced fluency.

Table 2.1. Characteristics of Learning Disabilities and Second Language Acquisition

Behaviors Associated With Learning Disabilities	Associated Behaviors With Acquiring a Second Language
Difficulty carrying out a series of directions, generally because of poor short-term memory or a lack of attention.	Difficulty carrying out a series of directions because • directions are not well understood • it can be harder to remember directions in a second language (Service, E., Simola, Metsänheimo, & Maury, 2002).
Difficulty with phonological awareness (i.e., distinguishing between or manipulating sounds auditorily), even though the student knows the sounds.	Difficulty distinguishing auditorily between unfamiliar sounds not in one's first language, or that are in a different order than in the first language.
Slow to learn sound-symbol correspondence; may seem to know letters' sounds one day but not the next.	Confusion with sound-symbol correspondence when it is different than in one's first language. Difficulty pronouncing sounds not in the first language.
Difficulty remembering sight words; may know word one day but not the next.	Difficulty remembering sight words when word meanings are not understood or when irregular patterns are used (e.g., *ea* can have both the long e and short e sounds).

Table 2.1. *(continued)*

Behaviors Associated With Learning Disabilities	Associated Behaviors With Acquiring a Second Language
Difficulty retelling a story in sequence. This may be because of poor short-term memory or retrieval skills.	Difficulty retelling a story in English without the expressive skills to do so. Yet the student might understand more than he or she can convey (i.e., receptive skills in English may be stronger than expressive skills).
Confusion with figurative language, idioms, and words with multiple meanings; students with LD might be very literal.	Confusion with figurative language, idioms, pronouns, conjunctions, and words with multiple meanings.
Slow to process challenging language.	Slow to process challenging language because it is not well understood.
May have poor auditory memory and not be able to repeat a string of sounds or words accurately.	May seem to have poor auditory memory if sounds or words are unfamiliar or not well understood.
May have difficulty concentrating.	Learning in a second language is mentally exhausting; therefore, ELLs may seem to have difficulty concentrating at times.
May seem easily frustrated and/or discouraged.	Learning in a second language can be frustrating.

ELLs at the **preproduction** stage typically develop a receptive vocabulary, but they do not yet speak their second language. During **early production**, ELLs are able to speak in short phrases of one or two words, and they also can memorize portions of language. Although ELLs generally have an expressive and receptive vocabulary of fewer than 1,000 words during this stage, during the **speech emergence** phase their vocabularies increase to around 3,000 words and they can communicate using simple questions and phrases. They may often make grammatical errors. At the **intermediate fluency** stage, ELLs have a vocabulary of around 6,000 words and can use more complicated sentence structures. They are also able to share their thoughts and opinions, although they may make frequent errors with more complicated sentence structures. The final stage is **advanced fluency**, which is typically reached after 5 to 10 years of learning the language; ELLs at this stage can function at a level close to native speakers.

Phonological and Phonemic Awareness

Phonological awareness is the ability to identify and manipulate the sounds in spoken language. A phoneme is a distinct unit of sound that distinguishes one word from another. For example, consider *bat*. If we change the /b/ to a /c/ or an /f/, we have a new word. The /b/, /c/, and /f/ are all phonemes. Phonemic awareness is a subcategory of phonological awareness, and refers to the ability to identify and manipulate the phonemes in spoken words. It is important to understand that phonemic awareness actually varies depending on the languages we speak (Antunez, 2002). We can only distinguish auditorily between sounds with which we have at least some familiarity (August & Shanahan, 2006). To help ELLs master the pronunciation of sounds not used in their native languages, they need to practice recognizing the sounds, then producing them. One way to do this is practice with *minimal pairs* (i.e., words that differ by one sound) to isolate the sound of interest, such as *pit/bit* and *pit/spit* (Kress, 2008). Table 2.2 provides examples of English sounds that are not used in other languages (Kress, 2008).

Table 2.2. English Sounds Not Used in Other Languages

Language	Sounds
Spanish	/dg/ /j/ /sh/ /th/ /z/
Chinese	/b/ /ch/ /d/ /dg/ /g/ /oa/ /sh/ /th/ /*th*/ /v/ /z/
French	/ch/ /ee/ /j/ /ng/ /oo/ /th/ /*th*/
Greek	/aw/ /ee/ /oo/ /e/
Italian	/a/ /*th*/ /ar/ /e/ /dg/ /h/ /ng/ /th/
Japanese	/dg/ /f/ /th/ /*th*/ /oo/ /v/

Phonological awareness is predictive of later reading ability (Ehri et al., 2001; Stahl & Murray, 1994). With Spanish-speaking ELLs, phonological awareness in Spanish or English appears to predict English reading achievement (Chiappe, Siegel, & Gottardo, 2002; Lindsey, Manis, & Bailey, 2003). Spanish phonological awareness might actually be a better predictor of English word reading than English or Spanish oral proficiency (Durgunoglu, Nagy, & Hancin-Bhatt, 1993).

Because phonological awareness is considered to be such a good predictor of later reading, it is an early indicator of possible reading problems and one way to identify students who may have LD. This is important because being able to provide early intervening services to students as a boost to their reading prowess can stave off later difficulties. Progress-monitoring tests such as the Dynamic Indicators of Basic Early Literacy Skills (DIBELS; Good & Kaminski, 2002) and AIMSweb (Shinn & Shinn, 2003) feature phonological awareness prominently. Yet for ELLs learning to read in English, phonological awareness tasks can be quite difficult when the student's home language does not include certain English phonemes (Antunez, 2002). For example, most dialects in Spanish do not distinguish between the /s/ and /z/ sounds (i.e., words with s and z both are pronounced as /s/, such as *silla* and *zapato*); most short vowel sounds in English do not exist in Spanish (e.g., /i/ and /u/). Japanese includes both the /l/ and /r/ sounds, but they are allophones (i.e., variants) of the same phoneme. Thus, Japanese speakers must learn to distinguish between these sounds. As noted earlier, students who are unfamiliar with certain sounds will not be able to distinguish these auditorily from other sounds. Also, pronouncing unfamiliar sounds is difficult. In general, phonological tasks become trickier.

Why is this so important? If teachers are not aware of these challenges, they might erroneously conclude that the ELL has a deficit in auditory discrimination or in phonological awareness. Teachers should keep in mind that confusion about sounds is normal and a natural byproduct of learning a new language. Make an effort to find out which phonemes are not present in your ELL students' home languages (see Kress, 2008) and help them develop the ability to discriminate between these new sounds. When assessing phonological awareness, use sounds you are sure the student knows. And, most important, do not erroneously draw the conclusion that the student has a disability without checking several other factors as part of a hypothesis-driven approach.

Alphabetic Principle

Whereas phonological awareness is only about the sounds in a language, the alphabetic principle adds the understanding of which letters make which sounds—or, as it is often called, *sound-symbol correspondence*. Learning the alphabetic principle in English can be challenging for ELLs, especially when they have not already learned to read in their first language or when their oral English proficiency is such that they do not understand many of the words they are reading. Reading can seem quite abstract and meaningless, for ELLs and other students. Many students will respond to the question "What is reading?" with, "Getting the words right." When we overemphasize correct word identification and underemphasize comprehension, we end up with many ELLs who are good "word callers": adept at identifying words without understanding their meaning (August & Shanahan, 2006; Crosson & Lesaux, 2009). But is that really reading?

In fact, Crosson and Lesaux (2009) found that the ELLs actually become slower readers as comprehension increases. This is the opposite of the expected relationship (i.e., generally fluency and comprehension are thought to be highly related).

When ELLs can already read in a home language, it is easier for them to learn to read in English. As the saying goes, "We only learn to read once." This is true whether we are monolingual, bilingual, or multilingual. Once we figure out how reading works, we can transfer that understanding to other languages. Yet even when we can read in one language, we must still learn the orthographic system of the new language. Thus, learning to read in a new language is easier when the orthographic systems are similar, such as with Italian or French, and much more difficult when they are not, as with Mandarin or Arabic.

The Importance of Schema

Learning and remembering new information is easier when we can connect it to what we already know. *Schema* means how our brains organize and store concepts we have previously learned. How can this help us with ELLs learning phonics? An important principle is that it is much more difficult to remember sounds and words that seem abstract and disconnected from previous learning. We learn best when we can connect new ideas with our existing knowledge. That is, instruction should build a bridge between previous knowledge and new learning. Yet, ELLs and other students are sometimes asked to learn sounds and letters in abstract ways. For example, consider Zoo-phonics, a frequently used means of teaching letter names and sounds to kindergartners. Zoo-phonics can be fun. Students like to get up and move around and be involved kinesthetically. Yet the names Queenie Quail, Umber Umbrella Bird, and Nigel Nightowl carry little meaning for students who have not already been exposed to them. Unless they learned them at home or in preschool, ELLs are being asked to learn new letter names and sounds along with new animal names and new people names. When we taught kindergarten ELLs, we asked them to bring in real objects from home that they knew well or used their names or items of clothing, such as boots/*botas* or popcorn/*palomitas de maiz*. As teachers, we tried to make these connections explicit. Otherwise, teachers may erroneously conclude that their ELLs must have LD or "can't learn to read," as we heard teachers say in a study of RTI at an elementary school trying RTI for the first time (Orosco & Klingner, 2010).

Effective Instruction for ELLs

The report from the National Literacy Panel on Language Minority Children and Youth (August & Shanahan, 2006) noted that oral language development should be considered an essential component of effective instruction for ELLs. Motivation is another factor that is critical for all students, and perhaps especially important for culturally and linguistically diverse students who are more likely to underachieve in schools across the country.

Oral Language Development

For ELLs, the challenge is not just how to provide explicit instruction in reading and writing, but also how to develop oral English proficiency. Oral language proficiency affects literacy acquisition (August & Shanahan, 2006). When students' oral language improves, so do their reading fluency and comprehension. Generic literacy programs are inadequate for ELLs because they guide teachers to explicitly teach only reading and writing skills, assuming that the prerequisite oral language skills are sufficiently under control (Gentile, 2004). Such programs neglect much needed explicit teaching for oral language development. To more successfully facilitate literacy acquisition of ELLs, Gentile (2004) recommended that literacy programs emphasize explicit teaching of both talk and text. *Oracy* is Gentile's term for literacy instruction that includes explicit teaching for literacy and oral language acquisition, as well as a focus on the child's culture and an emphasis on the importance of child-teacher interactions.

The less-than-full English oral proficiency of students who are becoming bilingual plays out in different ways. They are likely confused by English grammatical structures. They may need to strengthen their narration and retelling skills. They might not respond well to large group instruction, or they might refrain from contributing during whole class activities. They may have little understanding of the connections between oral and written language (Gentile, 2004).

It is important for teachers not to assume their ELLs have sufficient oral language proficiency to benefit from instruction. Harry and Klingner (2006) observed literacy instruction in classrooms with ELLs at beginning levels of English proficiency and noted that some teachers almost exclusively provided verbal explanations without the visual cues or other scaffolding that might have helped their instruction be more comprehensible to students. It was obvious to the observers that many students did not understand, yet teachers were likely to scold students for "not listening" or "not paying attention." One such teacher referred several of her students to the school's Child Study Team because she suspected they had LD, intellectual disability, or an emotional/behavioral disorder.

Teachers should observe their struggling learners closely to determine what their oral language needs might be. Francis and colleagues (2006) emphasized that "more structured 'talk' in classrooms across the U.S. would provide increased opportunities to informally assess students' oral language development in different contexts and for students to monitor and become more aware of, and active in, their own language development" (p. 28). A period of daily oracy instruction would be a logical addition to literacy and language acquisition. Examples of oracy instruction include explicit instruction or front-loading of vocabulary, sentence structures, and sentence transformations; building background knowledge and reviewing key ideas before and after reading; and providing many opportunities to practice oral language (e.g., through language experience approach, retelling stories with pictures).

Motivation

There is no doubt that the extent to which students are motivated affects their learning. Snow, Burns, and Griffin (1998) stressed that "motivation is crucial" (p. 3) to students learning to read, and noted that one of the principle reasons students struggle to learn to read is a loss of motivation. Frustration can lead to a lack of motivation, as can tasks that seem meaningless or disconnected from the realities of everyday life. Certainly many ELLs are faced with learning situations like this on a daily basis.

Rueda, MacGillivray, Monzó, and Arzubiaga (2001) emphasized the role of context and sociocultural factors in influencing reading engagement and motivation for ELLs. They noted that motivation is not only something the student brings to the learning situation, but also is an aspect of the task and a part of the learning environment. When ELLs seem to lack motivation, before teachers conclude that they do not want to learn, are lazy, or do not care, they should first look at factors such as whether the assignment is meaningful, relevant, and at an appropriate instructional level, and whether the students understand what is being asked of them and have all of the tools they need to accomplish the task.

What does a motivating program look like? Careful thought is given to the nature of the texts and activities used for instructing ELLs. The texts should be both interesting and at an appropriate level to nourish children's developing literacy and language skills. The topics, the relevancy, and the language all affect how children interact with the texts and how well they learn from them. Students bring linguistic and cultural resources to school that can be used to construct a relevant and engaging curriculum. Reading, writing, listening, and speaking should build upon these "funds of knowledge" (Moll & Greenberg, 1990). Instruction should account for the impact of culture and experience on cognition, literacy learning, behavior, oral language development, and motivation.

Conclusion

What should a teacher's first thought be when noticing a sign that could indicate an internal "deficit" in a child? Run with it, completing a referral form on the child for the school's problem-solving team? Or stop and wonder if there could be an alternative explanation? After all, the child is an ELL. Young ELLs have trouble distinguishing auditorily between phonemes that are not in their first language. Older students may be challenged by comprehension; they may be able to "word call" without understanding all of the vocabulary. Stop and question your intuitive reaction to why an ELL student might be struggling with any aspect of reading.

Focus Questions

- Name three reasons a student might have trouble retelling a story he or she has just read.

- Think back on ELLs you have referred to a problem-solving team in the past. Can you think of alternative explanations for any of the student's struggles?

- How do you think about motivation when you plan for, implement, and debrief following a lesson?

CHAPTER 3

What Are Some of the Different Types of ELLs and Why Are These Distinctions Important?

This chapter addresses:
- Definition of types of ELLS
- Why these distinctions are important
- What educators can do to understand and support the needs of diverse ELLs

Although ELLs have the shared experience of learning an additional language and culture, we need to be cognizant of the diversity of our students and be careful not to group them only by language proficiency or ethnic background. They bring so many diverse educational and lived experiences to our classrooms.

Types of ELLs

Sequential Versus Simultaneous Bilinguals

Sequential bilinguals first acquire one language in the home (L1) and then another language after they start school, or later (L2). On the other hand, *simultaneous bilinguals* acquire two or more languages at about the same time, from birth or early childhood (Baker, 2001). Experts differ on when the cut-off is for acquisition of the second language to begin and still be considered "simultaneous." The majority of ELLs in the United States are actually simultaneous bilinguals rather than sequential bilinguals. Immigrant students are more likely to be sequential bilinguals, whereas second and third generation ELLs are more likely to be simultaneous bilinguals. Although the majority of emerging bilinguals are considered simultaneous bilinguals, this is a concept we are still learning about, which, therefore, leaves room for misinterpretation of how and why ELLs progress as they do in school (Petrovic, 2010).

Long-Term ELLs

Long-term ELLs are students who have attended U.S. schools for 7 years or more and are still in need of language support. They tend to be orally bilingual, having social language, but limited in literacy and academic language in both their first and second language; this may be due to inconsistent schooling—a result of their moving back and forth between the United States and their country of origin or inconsistent instructional programming (Menken & Kleyn, 2009). Despite research showing the benefits of bilingual programs and fostering native language instruction (e.g., Goldenberg, 2008), most long-term ELLs have primarily received English instruction, some form of ESL or bilingual support that was inconsistent, or their instruction did not foster biliteracy (Menken & Kleyn, 2009). Long-term ELLs tend to have negative attitudes towards school due to their lack of success there. There is limited research on these students but, because a significant portion of our population of students fits this qualification, we need to understand how these students might follow a different learning trajectory than some of their peers.

To support long-term ELLs, we need to

- build a foundation by fostering native language instruction;
- focus on their strengths;
- recognize and respond to the gaps in education;
- focus on building academic skills rather than assuming students come to the new grade with previous grade-level skills;
- look at all areas of language proficiency data, not just oral language development;
- gather information from families about their attitudes and students' motivation toward school;
- plan content instruction that has embedded language development; and
- offer English language development classes for these students separate from newcomers.

Newcomers

Students newly arrived to the United States (less than 5 years) can vary in their past educational experiences (Freeman & Freeman, 2002). Some have had adequate formal schooling and can transfer academic concepts quickly, yet still score low on standardized tests. These students often need a focus on language support and catch up to their peers after a few years of language support. Other newcomers have had gaps in their education and therefore have limited academic proficiency in their native language. These students struggle in most areas of school and will need more time to learn language and content simultaneously.

To support newcomers

- ensure students are engaged in challenging curriculum and higher level thinking activities while developing language skills,
- help students understand the culture of school,
- understand the social-emotional side to adjusting to a new culture and language,
- understand students' educational backgrounds and home lives, and
- structure heterogeneous classroom activities so students can interact with peers and have peer language models.

Why Are These Distinctions Important?

The distinction between simultaneous and sequential bilinguals reminds us of the importance of **assessing bilingual students in both languages**. However, educators need to know how to interpret assessment data for emerging bilinguals. As described previously, relying on assessments that focus on parallel monolingualism can only give us limited information. How can we supplement that information through natural language samples, checklists, and informal assessments of language proficiency (see Chapter 10)? How can we document the bilingual trajectory of our students?

It is also important to **continuously monitor student language proficiency in both languages.** Many school districts only formally assess language development once a year—and only in English. How can we ensure we capture a student's full linguistic repertoire if we only have formal assessments in English? To counter this limited information, how can we progress monitor language development in both languages across the year?

Another aspect educators must consider is the student's **language history**; how educational experiences have played a role in the student's emerging bilingualism. Has one language been prioritized? Have students been in programs that were termed "bilingual" but did not focus on biliteracy? If an emerging bilingual student has moved across instructional programs, how has that affected language development? Was the student in a dual immersion program and transitioned to an English-only environment (or vice versa)?

Educators must consider the student's current **educational setting** and how language is viewed and incorporated into instruction (or not). How does the teacher foster native language development? Does the teacher promote cross-language metalinguistic skills even in an English-only program? Does the classroom environment promote biliteracy development?

Educators' **perceptions of bilingualism** may influence the way student work is assessed. Many ingrained beliefs about both students' oral language abilities and literacy achievement have been influenced by the "language as a problem" paradigm (Escamilla, 2000). Educators who do not have a solid understanding of types of bilingualism may be perpetuating this way of thinking. What is often perceived as low ability in both languages is often "typical' for simultaneous bilinguals. How can we focus on assets rather than deficits when analyzing student work?

Understanding the types of bilingualism and the types of ELLs we work with (see Table 3.1) is essential. This will not only help us better serve student needs, but perhaps also foster a more affirmative view of bilingualism and language differences.

Table 3.1. Types of English Language Learners

Types of ELLS	Distinctions
Simultaneous bilinguals	Were born in the United States but have grown up in households where a language other than English is spoken.
	Live in communities of speakers who primarily communicate in their L1 or go back and forth between languages.
	Have grown up being exposed to two languages simultaneously.
	May have not developed academic literacy in either L1 or L2.
	Often engage in extensive code-switching, thus making use of both linguistic systems to communicate.
	Have acquired oral proficiency in a language other than English first but may not have learned to read or write in that language.
Long-term ELLs	Have already spent more than 5 years in an English-speaking school.
	Have literacy skills that are below grade level.
	Have had some English as a Second Language classes or bilingual support.
	Require substantial and ongoing language and literacy support.

Table 3.1. *(continued)*

Types of ELLS	Distinctions
Newcomers with adequate formal schooling[a]	Have been in the country for fewer than 5 years.
	Have had an adequate degree of schooling in their native country.
	Perform in reading and writing at grade level.
	Find it relatively easy to catch up with their native-English-speaking peers.
	Have difficulty with standardized tests.
	Have parents who are educated speakers of their L1.
	Developed a strong foundation in their L1.
	Demonstrate the potential to make fast progress in English.
	Have found it easy to acquire a second or third language.
Newcomers with limited formal schooling	Have recently arrived in an English-speaking school (fewer than 5 years).
	Have experienced interrupted schooling.
	Have limited native-language and literacy skills.
	Perform poorly on achievement tasks.
	May not have had previous schooling.
	May experience feelings of loss of emotional and social networks.
	Have parents who have low literacy levels.
	Could have difficulty learning English.

Note. L1 = native or first language; L2 = second or additional language; ELL = English language learner.
[a]See Freeman & Freeman, 2002.

Currently the climate in many U.S. schools is such that language differences are problems that schools must "fix" and that they are the cause of much of the underachievement (Escamilla, 2000). False assumptions about bilingualism and language differences influence the instructional and assessment decisions we make for our ELLs. In a recent study of school-based RTI teams (Eppolito, 2011), we observed many conversations around decision making for ELLs, including intervention support and possible special education referrals.

Many observations were conducted in elementary schools offering bilingual programs. The school teams had specialists with expertise in second language acquisition and extensive knowledge about the students' backgrounds, families, and previous educational experiences. Therefore it was surprising for us to hear so many negative comments about language (see Table 3.2). So many educators alluded to students' lack of English proficiency as the reason for continued academic failure. We noticed that it was not central to just one team member, but multiple members of the team used this type of deficit language. What is problematic about these statements? Consider the attitude toward emerging bilingualism that they reflect; how might such attitudes affect decisions about students' needs? Failing to address and confront this deficit paradigm of bilingualism places ELLs at a continuing disadvantage, misdirects our efforts, and takes away the opportunity for our students to become bilingual and biliterate.

Table 3.2. Statements Reflecting a Deficit View of Bilingualism

Educator	Comment
Third-grade teacher	She really has a language problem, don't you think? A second language problem? I see her trying but a lot of it is her language; she can't say some of the words we are reading because of the language problem.
ESL teacher	His mom only speaks Spanish. His dad speaks English very well. He's probably conversing most of the time in Spanish because I bet dad lapses into Spanish at home because it's the common language.
Second-grade teacher	It's a language issue because Mom doesn't speak any English at all....I see her lapsing, she'll be talking and then all of the sudden she is talking in Spanish.
First-grade teacher	She's second language. She went back and forth, Spanish–English, so language is a problem. Mom supports her but she speaks all Spanish.
Principal	That kid is lower than a lot of your other kids that are heavily impacted with language.

Note. Adapted with permission from A. Eppolito, *The Response to Intervention Decision-Making Process for English Language Learners: Three Elementary School Case Studies* (Doctoral Dissertation, 2011).

Conclusion

Understanding the diversity among ELLs will better help us consider the strengths they bring to our classrooms and also to address the potential challenges they might encounter. Knowing how students have developed their language proficiency in both their native languages and English, as well as their past educational experiences, can provide insights into their learning trajectories. Hopefully we can then avoid some of the common pitfalls and false assumptions about what is influencing their learning.

Focus Questions

- Think of some ways you can learn about the previous educational and language experiences of the ELLs in your classroom or school (e.g., Can you develop a home language survey or interview for the families of your students?).

- How will you utilize this background information in your classroom or school to make instructional or assessment decisions for your ELLs?

- Explore the perception of bilingual students at your school.

CHAPTER 4

What Does It Mean to Consider "Opportunity to Learn" When Determining Whether Students May Have LD?

This chapter addresses:
- Implementation of culturally and linguistically responsive instruction in all tiers of instruction
- High-quality core instruction for ELLs that involves research-based promising practices
- High-quality Tier 2 and Tier 3 instruction with tier alignment
- Process for ensuring opportunity to learn

Some ELLs are inappropriately identified as having LD not because they have disabilities, but rather because they have not received an adequate opportunity to learn. Federal and state special education laws specify that a lack of opportunity to learn must be ruled out before a disability determination can be made (IDEA, 2006). Therefore, looking at the quality of instruction ELLs receive is a necessary first step when deciding whether to pursue an evaluation for possible special education placement. To determine whether instruction is appropriate, we must look into classrooms and ensure they are culturally and linguistically responsive and foster promising practices for ELLs. High-quality instruction for ELLs ensures access to the curriculum, is interactive and meaningful, and develops both content knowledge and language skills.

Many schools are moving toward using a multitiered instructional and assessment model such as response to intervention (RTI) in their programing to implement instruction, monitor progress, and refer students for potential LD identification and special education placement. The key components of the RTI model include high-quality instruction matched to the needs of students, evidence-based interventions of increasing intensity, ongoing progress monitoring, and data-driven decision making (Hoover, 2008; Klingner, Hoover, & Baca, 2008). The RTI model is both a prevention and an intervention model of instruction. All students are screened and identified as at risk for learning difficulties in reading. Those students who are struggling in the classroom are provided interventions of increasing intensity in the mainstream classroom and through small group instruction before being considered for special education referral. Progress is closely monitored and documented at all stages of the process. Decisions on where to place students are based on the data collected from multiple sources. The majority of students' needs will ideally be met through this process, and only those who are not responding at a certain designated rate and duration are referred for potential learning disabilities. When we talk about high quality, culturally responsive instruction for ELLs, we must consider what that looks like in all tiers of the RTI model and how high quality core instruction must be verified for ELLs first and foremost.

Culturally and Linguistically Responsive Instruction

Culturally responsive instruction (Gay, 2000; Ladson-Billings, 1994) foregrounds instruction based on the cultural knowledge, prior experiences and knowledge, performance styles and strengths, language proficiency, home language background, and sociocultural background of each student. Teaching considers not only students' ethnic backgrounds but also each student's prior experiences, including knowledge to make learning more appropriate and effective. Culturally responsive literacy instruction also includes choosing relevant multicultural literature and other reading materials to which the student can personally relate (including youth experiences unrelated to ethnicity). Programs that are culturally responsive tap into community resources that promote school community partnerships. Teachers who are culturally responsive (Villegas & Lucas, 2002) not only instruct from a culturally and linguistically responsive framework but also build relationships with their students through creating caring environments. Students who are connected through a caring and trusting relationship with the teacher are more motivated to learn and to succeed (Nieto, 2004). Students also work harder when they feel their teachers care for them both personally and academically (Alder, 2002; Klingner et al., 2006). Culturally responsive teachers believe ELLs enter the schooling environment with a wealth of experiences and language tools. According to Brown and Doolittle, "The child's language and culture should not be viewed as a liability but as an asset—strength with which to build an education" (2008, p. 2).

Classroom examples: A group of teachers discovered that their students, who were native speakers of Hawaiian Creole, were struggling with various mathematics concepts (Brenner, 1998). The teachers and researchers interviewed parents and observed students in their home settings and realized that students had mathematical knowledge upon which they could draw. So the teachers began approaching their curriculum differently. They rearranged the curriculum so the concepts taught first were the ones that built on students' strengths (e.g., counting rather than vocabulary related to position of objects). They taught the vocabulary in students' native language, and also activities in the classroom to be more authentic and familiar to students (e.g., students ran a student store to understand money, teachers included cooking activities of native cuisine). They saw dramatic increases in student academic success in mathematics.

Arce (2000) similarly describes a culturally responsive bilingual first-grade classroom in which the teacher integrated social studies with literacy instruction in a unit about shelters around the world. Throughout the unit of study the students researched

> factors influencing architectural styles of shelters, such as weather, geography, topography, economy, and other available resources. They designed shelters through collaborative activities, decided how to identify rooms in their buildings, and brought items from their homes to furnish the shelters....This classroom was a busy community where one heard a constant buzzing of voices. Students worked independently in small groups of two, three, or four, while the adults (researcher, teacher, Spanish- and English-speaking parents who volunteered during different language blocks) worked with groups or individuals....Throughout the day children were encouraged to talk. Sometimes they needed to be reminded to talk about the task at hand, but they were rarely asked to stop talking. (p. 254)

High-Quality Instruction for ELLs

High-quality instruction for ELLs should include the five standards for effective pedagogy developed by the Center for Research on Education, Diversity and Excellence (Doherty et al., 2002):

- teachers and students producing together,
- developing language and literacy across the curriculum,
- making lessons meaningful,
- teaching complex thinking, and
- teaching through conversation.

These five standards have been shown to be effective in the education of learners by reducing achievement gaps between diverse and mainstream students (Doherty et al., 2002). In addition, effective instruction must place a focus on oral language development. Oral language proficiency in English is essential to developing proficiency in reading and writing, and oral proficiency in the student's native or first language facilitates this process (August & Shanahan, 2006). Students also must have opportunities to use language in authentic ways (e.g., flexible grouping structures, complex instruction with heterogeneous grouping to allow for peer modeling).

Literacy Instruction

Specific to literacy instruction, Short and Fitzsimmons (2007) identified the following effective teaching practices: (a) integrate listening, speaking, reading, and writing skills; (b) teach components and processes of reading and writing; (c) teach reading comprehension strategies; (d) focus on vocabulary development; (e) build and activate background knowledge; (f) teach language through content and themes; and (g) use the native language strategically. It has been shown that direct approaches (explicit and focused teaching) and interactive approaches to teaching reading and writing are more effective than process-based approaches alone. Process-based approaches (reading and writing workshops, sustained silent reading) emphasize more inductive learning (Genesee & Riches, 2006).

Because literacy is so complex, providing literacy instruction that is socially appropriate, culturally responsive, and intellectually stimulating can be challenging. There are, however, instructional strategies that allow for differentiation of core literacy instruction and support literacy development for ELLs in all the domains of literacy (Klingner, Soltero-González, & Lesaux, 2010; see Table 4.1), while also incorporating all four language modalities and making direct and appropriate connections to children's native language.

Table 4.1. Domains of Literacy

Domains	Instructional Strategies
Oral language	ELLs need time to verbalize their thinking as well as have an opportunity to listen to others' ideas about particular topics. Students' oral language fluency can be enhanced by deliberately providing opportunities for students to interact with each other around the content. Strategies that build background knowledge, language experience approach, role play, storytelling using wordless books, songs and chants, think-pair-share, table talk, and other forms of academic discourse allow students to socially construct meaning and develop their oral language skills. Strategies that promote oral language development must be explicitly planned and incorporated throughout the school day.

Table 4.1 *(continued)*

Domains	Instructional Strategies
Word work	Although the main purpose of word-work activities is to build foundational literacy skills, these activities should be done in meaningful and interactive ways and in the context of reading and writing activities, rather than in isolation. Consider working on phonics with ELLs using familiar sounds, words, and phrases. Working with words that are produced by the students themselves is very valuable because they are already familiar with the meaning of the word or phrases and are able to focus on phonemic awareness (segmenting, blending, syllabication, onset-rime, initial/final sound) in meaningful ways. ELLs sometimes have difficulty transferring sight words to real reading when their only exposure to sight words has been in isolation. Peer or teacher dictations provide a meaningful activity for word work.
Fluency	Fluency is the ability to read quickly and accurately while maintaining "meaning-full" phrasing. Two common ways of improving reading fluency are repeated oral reading and independent silent reading. Other strategies include modeled and shared reading with patterned language books, Readers' Theatre, partner reading, and reading with audiobooks. Strategies that incorporate technology (e.g., voice recorders) allow students to hear themselves read and to evaluate their own fluency.
Comprehension	For ELLs, it is important to provide instruction that enhances their comprehension by building background knowledge, highlighting key vocabulary, and interacting socially to make meaning. Some of the challenges that ELLs may face in reading comprehension are related to language proficiency, vocabulary knowledge, background knowledge, and use of comprehension strategies.

Table 4.1 *(continued)*

Domains	Instructional Strategies
Cross-language connections	Culturally and linguistically responsive teaching considers students' linguistic toolkit. Strategies that explicitly connect one language to another, noting similarities and differences, enhance comprehension. Using students' L1 enhances English language acquisition. Knowledge of what literacy-related skills and experiences ELLs have in L1 and L2 allows teachers to build on students' strengths and needs, promotes metalinguistic awareness, and leverages the students' L1. The use of cognates, bilingual books, and explicit comparisons are ways to heighten cross-language connections.
Writing	Helping students to make connections between oral and written language is very important in the beginning stages of second-language literacy development. These activities should be meaningful and functional. Guided writing, modeled writing, interactive writing, and collaborative writing are strategies that help ELLs at various levels of English proficiency. Some strategies incorporate oral language practice before writing occurs, allowing students to verbalize their thinking before putting it into writing. Other times, students share orally with a partner after they have thought about a topic and written about it. Proofreading, editing, and revising may be difficult for students to perform; their proficiency at editing depends on students' language proficiency in English. Often we may ask ELLs to tell us if something they wrote "sounds right." Determining if something "sounds right" requires fluency in English. Many ELLs may struggle with editing their own writing when correctness obscures the expression of meaning and the development of complex ideas (Cloud et al., 2009). Cloud (2009) and her colleagues (2009) suggest using writing rubrics and the "six traits" model to guide students in editing their own writing. Another way to address editing is through the language experience approach (Nessel & Dixon, 2008) and other forms of interactive writing. It is important to guide ELLs as they learn aspects of proofreading in a social and nonthreatening atmosphere.

Table 4.1 *(continued)*

Domains	Instructional Strategies
Connections to home and community	Literacy that deliberately connects students' homes and local communities to classroom instruction is what Moll and colleagues (1992) called "funds of knowledge." Learning and literacy for ELLs are enhanced when the practices and knowledge of the students and their families are incorporated into the classroom. Storytelling about family and neighborhoods, autobiographies and personal narratives, books (written, audiotaped), friendly letters to family and friends, research projects in the local community, and lessons or units that draw from students' local literacy practices and knowledge are but a few strategies that help make connections to the home and community.

Note. Adapted with permission from "Response to Intervention for English Language Learners," by J. K. Klingner, L. Soltero-González, and N. Lesaux, in *Successful Approaches to Response to Intervention (RTI): Collaborative Practices for Improving K-12 Literacy* (p. 146). Copyright 2010 International Reading Association. ELL = English language learner; L1 = native or first language; L2 = second or additional language.

Mathematics Instruction

Similar to literacy, achieving proficiency in mathematics relies on appropriate, effective and culturally responsive instruction with adequate opportunity to learn. There is evidence that early intervention can prevent mathematic difficulties for many learners, including ELLs. Many students who struggle with reading may also struggle with mathematics due to the academic language embedded in the instruction and curriculum. There is the need to distinguish struggling mathematics learners whom may need more language support from those with true LD. Although mathematics has received less attention than reading, researchers have been paying attention in more recent years and have come up with the following recommendations for ELLs (Francis et al., 2006):

1. ELLs need early, explicit, and intensive instruction and intervention in basic mathematics concepts and skills.

2. Academic language is as central to mathematics as it is to other academic areas. It is a significant source of difficulty for many ELLs who struggle with mathematics.

3. ELLs need academic language support to understand and solve the word problems that are often used for mathematics assessment and instruction.

Students benefit from culturally responsive classwide mathematics instruction followed by supplementary explicit instruction for those who need more support. Francis and colleagues (2006) outlined the many ways that ELLs need support with the language of mathematics instruction. Many words in mathematics have multiple meanings in everyday conversation, but they have different and specific meanings when working through math concepts (e.g., point, plot, root, column). Additionally, there are phrases specific to mathematics with which children may need a lot of instructional support in order to understand and apply independently (e.g., least common denominator, square root). English language learners may also struggle with the formatting of textbooks. They need support to understand the symbols, positioning of symbols and graphics, and multiple meanings of words. The use of tools and hands-on manipulatives is helpful for ELLs, but does not replace the need for language support. It is recommended to use structured discussions, retells, and think-alouds to explain strategy use and problem solving. Teachers must approach every lesson considering what language students need to accomplish the tasks and activities and integrate both content and language objectives. Word problems are pervasive in mathematics and therefore deserve specific attention. As mentioned previously, the language of mathematics, including word problems, is very specific and ELLs need to understand what the words specifically mean in addition to understanding the content that the statements are addressing. It is necessary for teachers to determine a student's prerequisite skills to understand a word problem and the prior knowledge the student has (both procedural and factual knowledge).

Support for ELLs Across Instructional Tiers

Another aspect of ensuring students have had opportunity to learn is ensuring that ELLs receive tiered support that is linked to classroom instruction and that also focuses on language development. Too often we see boxed intervention programs that focus only on isolated literacy skills such as phonics or fluency. If ELLs are placed in these programs without individualized support or language development, they are not being provided an optimal opportunity to learn. Additionally, the intervention should be made to support what is being taught in core instruction. Although some interventions for monolingual speakers are beneficial for ELLs (Gersten et al., 2007), the same principles of culturally responsive instruction must be applied to interventions, and often they need to be adjusted to support ELLs. Students need opportunities to develop oral language and utilize their native language, or they might need explicit direct teaching of skills combined with interactive activities in order to process heavy cognitive load.

Literacy Instructional Approaches and Interventions

Similar to Tier 1 core instruction, Tier 2 and 3 interventions should be research-based for ELLs and instructionally, culturally, and linguistically responsive and appropriate. The language of instruction when implementing interventions should match that of Tier 1. In other words, students who are receiving native language literacy or mathematics instruction as part of a bilingual or dual-language program should also participate in native language interventions. When ELLs show little growth in response to these supplemental, intensive interventions, the problem-solving team must decide whether to continue Tier 2 instruction for a short time longer, alter Tier 2 instruction (i.e., try something new), or discontinue it. When students seem to be progressing well, presumably they no longer need Tier 2 instruction. There are some students, however, whose progress diminishes when this supplemental support is taken away. When this happens, there is no reason not to provide it again. On the other hand, when students still do not seem to be doing well, even after their teachers and support personnel have tried several different interventions, it may be appropriate to provide them with ongoing intensive support in Tier 3. Instruction at Tier 3 is even more focused and personalized, and has a longer duration than instruction at Tier 2.

Several research studies in recent years have demonstrated the potential of Tier 2 interventions that combine oral language instruction, phonological awareness, word study, vocabulary, fluency, and listening and reading comprehension to improve reading for ELLs who seem to be experiencing reading difficulties in kindergarten, first, and second grades (Linan-Thompson, Bryant, Dickson, & Kouzekanani, 2005; Linan-Thompson, Vaughn, Hickman-Davis, & Kouzekanani, 2003; Linan-Thompson, Vaughn, Prater, & Cirino, 2006; Vaughn, Cirino, et al., 2006; Vaughn, Linan-Thompson, et al., 2006a, 2006b; Vaughn, Mathes, et al., 2005). The duration of the interventions seems to make a difference, with longer interventions probably more effective than shorter interventions. Also, it appears to be very helpful to emphasize oral language development, English-language acquisition, and listening comprehension, components that seem to be especially important for ELLs. Table 4.2 describes effective instruction and interventions for ELLs.

Mathematics Instructional Approaches and Interventions

In addition to literacy interventions, researchers have identified strategies and recommendations for early intervention in mathematics instruction. Similar to literacy instruction, it is recommended that students are screened for potential problems in

Table 4.2. Core Instruction (Tier 1) and Strategic Literacy Interventions (Tier 2) for ELLs in Grades K–3

Research Study	Instruction	Intervention
Language experience approach (LEA; Nessel & Dixon, 2008)	1 story weekly, working with same text for 1 week Targets emergent skills, readiness, word work, fluency	LEA is a reading method based on students' own language. Students as authors dictate a story about an actual experience to a scribe, who may be a teacher, a teaching assistant, a parent or community volunteer, or a tutor. Next they copy the story (or trace it), illustrate it, and read it again and again. For ELLs, this approach allows for vocabulary development and phonemic awareness in context, based on interests and prior knowledge; therefore can be culturally responsive, helps make connections between oral and written language.
Dictado (Escamilla, Geisler, Hopewell, Sparrow, & Butvilofsky, 2009)	15–20 min/day, at least 3 times a week Targets oral language, fluency, cross-linguistic connections	*Dictado* is a cross-language method addressing receptive and expressive language skills: • The teacher purposefully creates a meaningful text as the focus for teaching, spelling, grammar, and language arts, and dictates sentences to students. • Students write in pencil or blue/black pen, and then teacher and students collaboratively create a corrected model of the text while students self-correct using red pencil and standard markings. This approach helps ELLs attend to similarities and differences across languages; cross-language transfer allows students to draw from both languages and utilize their native language.

Table 4.2 *(continued)*

Research Study	Instruction	Intervention
Collaborative strategic reading (CSR; Klingner & Vaughn, 1999)	1–2 times/week Targets comprehension, word work	CSR is a multicomponent reading comprehension strategy that teaches students metacognitive awareness when reading complex texts. It can be used with both narrative and expository text. • Students work in groups with assigned roles to interact with a text. • Teachers lead students through text preview (predicting, brainstorming, key vocabulary), then students lead each other through reading activities (word work, main idea) and after reading activities (questioning and summarizing). • The teacher then leads a wrap-up section. CSR promotes oral language development, interacting with text in meaningful context, and use of native language.
Peer-assisted learning strategies (PALS; Fuchs, Fuchs, & Burish, 2000)	25–35-minute activities implemented 2–4 times/week Targets fluency, comprehension	PALS is supplemental reading activity that pairs an average or high reader with a lower reader. Pairs of learners are selected on the basis of their reading fluency scores and pairs read together for approximately 4 weeks. Stronger readers support the efforts of those who are struggling through partner reading, retelling, paragraph shrinking, and prediction relay. PALS reading materials are geared toward the lower reading level in each pair; implementation of PALS facilitates peer interactions and immediate corrective feedback. For ELLs, PALS promotes oral language development and provides a peer model for fluency development and feedback (see Saenz, Fuchs, & Fuchs, 2005).

Table 4.2 *(continued)*

Research Study	Instruction	Intervention
Modified Guided Reading (Avalos, Plasencia, Chavez, & Rascón, 2007)	2+ days a week for 20–30 minutes Targets fluency, comprehension, word work	Uses the same structure as guided reading but with modifications that benefit ELLs. Emphasizes the importance of text selection and anticipating common stumbling blocks for ELLs. • Teacher presents culturally relevant text through a guided discussion connecting the content and language structure to students' personal lives (e.g., picture walk, predicting). • Teacher reads guided reading text aloud to model fluency and generate discussion regarding comprehension and vocabulary guided by the teacher and students. • ELLs with higher L2 oral proficiency vocalize softly as they read the text. • Teacher observes and coaches students by reinforcing correct strategies and using word recognition prompts to problem solve. • Word work focuses on morphological awareness and phonological awareness connected to guided reading text. • Vocabulary journals and writing assignments connect to guided reading text. Authentic use of language rather than isolated, detailed vocabulary instruction that targets ELLs' needs, while incorporating culturally relevant text.

Table 4.2 *(continued)*

Research Study	Instruction	Intervention
Graphic organizers	Daily Targets word work, comprehension	Graphic organizers (e.g., tree diagrams, semantic maps, concept maps, word maps) help students organize key topics or concepts and make connections among new vocabulary and concepts in reading material.
		Teacher provides direction in the development and use of one or more graphic organizers, then students work in small groups to develop their own.
		When used as a targeted intervention for preteaching in reading, graphic organizers assist learners to activate prior knowledge and put into context new vocabulary and concepts that are directly connected to new reading material. Use of graphic organizers provides learners opportunity to personalize their reading.
		Graphic organizers help make language visual for ELLS, can be used to frontload vocabulary or concepts, and can help build background knowledge.

Note. ELL = English language learner; L2 = second or additional language.

mathematics, identified as at-risk, and then provided targeted supplemental instruction. Gersten and colleagues (2009) found evidence for the following practices:

- Instructional materials for students receiving interventions should focus intensely on in-depth treatment of whole numbers in kindergarten through Grade 5 and on rational numbers in Grades 4 through 8. These materials should be selected by committee.

- Instruction during the intervention should be explicit and systematic. This includes providing models of proficient problem solving, verbalization of thought processes, guided practice, corrective feedback, and frequent cumulative review.

- Interventions should include instruction on solving word problems that is based on common underlying structures.

- Intervention materials should include opportunities for students to work with visual representations of mathematical ideas and interventionists should be proficient in the use of visual representations of mathematical ideas.

- Interventions at all grade levels should devote about 10 minutes in each session to building fluent retrieval of basic arithmetic facts.

- Monitor the progress of students receiving supplemental instruction and other students who are at risk.

Ensuring Opportunity to Learn

In addition to ensuring quality classroom instruction, we should examine classroom progress-monitoring data sets to look for patterns in student performance. If most ELLs or similar peers are thriving, then it is likely that instruction is appropriate. If most ELLs are showing little progress, then instruction needs to be changed to better meet their language and learning needs. Some ELLs are taught in "disabling contexts," with too few opportunities to receive appropriate instruction matched to their needs and too few opportunities to develop their oral language and literacy skills. For example, in a recent study of a diverse school implementing RTI for the first time, Orosco and Klingner (2010) observed many of the teachers providing inadequate instruction to ELLs. Teachers did not consider students' language proficiency, build on their background knowledge, or connect instruction to their home lives, and much of the instruction was out of context and inaccessible for students.

As part of a multitiered system of support, school leadership teams should incorporate a process for measuring the adequacy of core instruction. This process should include tools and forms for analyzing student class data sets in addition to observation protocols to ensure culturally responsive practices in Tier 1. Teams can then decide if additional classroom observations are needed when students are suspected of struggling. This topic is discussed further in Chapter 7.

As part of our long-term REME project (RTI Effectiveness Model for ELLs; see http://mdcc.sri.com/cohort5_co.html), partnering with two schools with a high population of ELLs, we developed a culturally and linguistically diverse (CLD) guide to be used with RTI. The guide can be used for instructional coaching, documenting observations of Tier 1 instruction, professional development, and curriculum planning. We have recommended that teachers start with specific research-based strategies that provide the most bang for your buck. For example, some of our recommendations include daily *dictados* (Escamilla et al., 2009), strategies to promote interactive learning for oral language development (Herrera, Perez, & Escamilla, 2010), use of authentic texts, use of the language experience approach (LEA; Nessel & Dixon, 2008) and collaborative strategic reading (CSR; Klingner, Vaughn, Boardman, & Swanson, 2012).

We worked with school-based teams to ensure teachers were consistently using these strategies, and how they can document these and utilize that information to make valid decisions.

Conclusion

According to Spinelli (2008), we need to "begin assessing the instructional program prior to assessing the child" (p. 106). We must consider a student's opportunity to learn and the many complex contextual factors that influence their learning. We cannot say with confidence a student is or is not responding to instruction unless we ensure they are engaged in learning opportunities that are culturally and linguistically responsive and founded on best practices for ELLs across all tiers of instruction.

Focus Questions

- Write down some of the ways your practice is culturally and linguistically responsive. Are there aspects of your practice you would like to make more effective for ELLs?

- Discuss how well your tiered instruction is aligned with core instruction and how this process could be streamlined in your classroom or school.

- Write down literacy and math interventions you have seen work well for ELLs. Choose one Tier 2 intervention suggestion from this chapter and describe how you can incorporate it into your practice.

- How can your school team ensure opportunity to learn for ELLs?

CHAPTER 5

What Are Some Common Misconceptions About ELLs and the Second Language Acquisition Process? What Are the Realities?

This chapter addresses:
- What it means to be bilingual
- Assessing ELLs' full linguistic repertoire
- Providing instruction that enables ELLs to draw on all of their linguistic knowledge

Several misconceptions about the second language acquisition process affect the instruction ELLs receive and the decisions made about them. McLaughlin (1992) referred to these as "what every teacher needs to unlearn". Educators should have at least a basic understanding of the theories of language acquisition and how the intersections of language and learning influence the learning trajectories of ELLs. Misconceptions about language and literacy development can perpetuate a deficit view of ELLs' ability to learn. When this happens, ELLs' language proficiencies in other languages become seen as a problem to be fixed rather than an asset to build on.

We know a lot about bilingualism and the second language acquisition process (e.g., Baca & Cervantes, 2004; Bialystok, 2001; Collier, 2005; Cummins, 1986, 1989; Grabe, 2009; Grosjean & Li, 2013; Valdés & Figueroa, 1994). This chapter draws upon the vast research literature to offer positive and constructive solutions to the challenges teachers and others face in their schools and classrooms with emerging bilingual students. Table 5.1 highlights some common misconceptions and realities and presents implications for each.

Misconception: Bilingualism Means Equal Proficiency in Both Languages

Bilingualism and what it means to be bilingual continue to be misunderstood by the education community at large. In the U.S. public school system, ELLs are a diverse group and include children who were born in countries around the world, as well as those born in the United States. English language learners' linguistic proficiencies in their multiple

Table 5.1. Misconceptions and Realities About the Language Acquisition Process

Misconception	Reality	Implications
Bilingualism means equal proficiency in both languages.	Bilingualism rarely means equal proficiency in both languages.	ELLs include students with a wide range of proficiencies in their home language and English, with varying levels of bilingualism. Bilingual students may be stronger in some areas in their home language and stronger in other areas in English.
Semilingualism is a valid concept and "non-non" classifications indicating children are limited in their home language and English (based on test results) are useful categories.	*Semilingualism* and "non-non" categories are the results of tests that do not measure the full range and depth of language proficiencies among ELLs acquiring two languages simultaneously.	The vast majority of children begin school having acquired the syntactic and morphological rules of the language of their community. Current language assessment measures rarely capture the full range of skills that bilingual children bring to the classroom. Classifying students as "limited-limited" or "non-non" is not useful because it does not reveal what students know or need to learn; instead, it promotes low expectations. Other forms of authentic assessment should be used to determine language proficiency levels of ELLs, including natural language samples.

Table 5.1 *(continued)*

Misconception	Reality	Implications
The more time students spend receiving English literacy instruction (immersed in it), the faster they will learn to read in English.	Students who receive some home language literacy instruction achieve at higher levels in English reading than students who do not receive it.	Instruction in English and interactions with English speakers are important, but not enough to provide the optimal support for ELLs to be able to fully participate in classroom learning and achieve to their potential. Skills developed in students' native language transfer to English, particularly when teachers help students make connections across languages. Students acquire English when they receive input that is understandable (i.e., by using language in context, providing background knowledge, using visual and context cues, clarifying vocabulary).
Errors are problematic and should be avoided.	"Errors" are a positive sign that the student is making progress and are a necessary aspect of second language acquisition.	*Interlanguage*—overgeneralizing grammatical rules from one language to another—is a natural, normal aspect of second language acquisition. Errors such as confusion with verb tenses, plurals, possessives, word order, subject–verb agreement, and the use of articles are common among ELLs and should not be interpreted as signifying that a student has a disability. *Code switching* is common among bilingual individuals around the world and should not be considered a sign of confusion.

Table 5.1 *(continued)*

Misconception	Reality	Implications
All ELLs learn English in the same way at about the same rate; a slow rate of acquisition indicates a possible disability.	The length of time it takes students to acquire academic language in English varies a great deal, from 4 to 7 years or more.	Many different variables affect the language acquisition process. Even when ELLs appear to be quite proficient in English, they may not yet have acquired full academic proficiency. The reasons for an ELL's struggles when learning to read are more likely to relate to the language acquisition process than a disability.
ELLs are not ready to engage in higher level thinking until they learn basic skills.	ELLs are as capable of engaging in higher level thinking as their fully proficient peers.	Instruction and practice at every grade level must provide frequent opportunities for ELLs to engage in higher level thinking. Instruction should ensure that ELLs of all proficiency levels have multiple entry points to access content.
Parents and other caregivers should speak English in the home instead of their first language so that ELLs have more exposure to English.	Perhaps the most important way caregivers can help is to speak their home language so that their children grow up with lots of language and are able to communicate with their extended family and others.	It is not about which language, but about building language, any language. Families should talk and talk in the languages in which they are the most comfortable as a way to build their children's literacy skills and knowledge of the world. Building knowledge in any language facilitates thinking and comprehension. Once one knows a concept, adding an English label is relatively simple.

Note. Adapted with permission from "Misconceptions About the Second Language Acquisition Process," by J. Klingner, E. Almanza de Schonewise, C. de Onis, L. Méndez Barletta, and J. Hoover, in *English Language Learners Who Struggle With Reading: Language Acquisition or Learning Disabilities?* (p. 17). Copyright 2008 by Corwin Press. ELL = English language learner; "non-non" classifications indicate children are limited or low achieving in their home language and in English.

languages vary. Their total proficiency should be considered to be the sum of proficiencies in their multiple languages, or, to put it another way, their full linguistic repertoire. They may be stronger in some language components in one language and more proficient in other domains in English, depending on how and where they learn English and the language(s) of instruction in school (Klingner et al., 2010).

Bilingualism means knowing two languages rather than one, whereas *multilingualism* means knowing multiple languages. A commonly held view considers bilinguals to be "only those able to function as native speakers of each of their two languages" (Valdés & Figueroa, 1994, p. 7). Valdés and Figueroa (1994) disagreed with this perspective, however, explaining that, in reality, very few people attain a level of bilingualism where they achieve native-like proficiency in both languages (see Chapter 3 for more information on different types of bilingualism). Valdés and Figueroa emphasized that bilingualism seldom signifies equal proficiency in two languages. Similarly, Takakuwa (2003) noted that the distinction between being bilingual and monolingual is a matter of degree along a continuum, rather than an absolute discrete difference.

Equivalent bilingualism implies that students are surrounded by multiple languages, yet rarely are homes and schools balanced linguistic environments. Any given individual is likely to use languages differently in various locations, for different functions (Valdés & Figueroa, 1994). For instance, a student may know science terms better in English than in Vietnamese because he is learning in English in school, but knows more everyday language in Vietnamese.

Bilingualism is multifaceted and complex. Therefore, Valdés and Figueroa (1994) advocated for a more expansive definition of bilingualism that encompasses these complexities, preferring "a common human condition in which an individual possesses more than one language competence. . .that makes it possible to. . .function at some level in more than one language" (p. 8). This definition emphasizes competence and the ability to function at some level in more than one language. Yet, in schools across the United States, starting kindergarten speaking only one language is considered the norm; knowing more than one language is believed to be abnormal and a problem. In other words, rather than ELLs being perceived as potential or emerging bilinguals, they are labeled as "limited" in English. Yet, what if the standard was to know more than one language (as it is in many countries around the world)? Then it would be those who only speak one language who would be considered "limited" (Klingner, Almanza de Schonewise, de Onis, Méndez Barletta, & Hoover, 2008).

Misconception: *Semilingualism* Is a Valid Concept and Non-Non Classifications Are Useful Categories

Many beginning special education teachers initially buy into the idea that some students are low-achieving in both English and Spanish—they certainly test that way—and reason that ELLs have not received sufficient opportunities to fully develop their language. Some teachers may even wonder if that is why these students are struggling to learn to read. This kind of attitude about speaking a home language other than English is thought-provoking, because it appears to vary depending on both what the language is and the socioeconomic status of the family. If a student comes from a middle or upper middle class background and speaks French at home, it is unlikely that we will worry about her ability to learn English. Yet if she comes from a low socioeconomic background and speaks Spanish, we may think of her home language as a "problem" or obstacle to learning English. When the language that ELLs bring to school is deemed to be "low" level, particularly among children from low-income families, educators are more likely to blame the child or the family when the student does not thrive (Harry & Klingner, 2006).

MacSwan and Rolstad (2006) identified two reasons for this. One is that our current language assessment system is flawed: The tests we use are not able to accurately assess an individual's full linguistic repertoire. Assessments are designed to assess a student's mastery of languages independent from one another, as if each language occupies a different, separate space in the brain, and to compare the student's performance with that of monolingual speakers in each language as a point of reference. Yet languages do not operate in separate spaces; rather, they function together (Grosjean & Li, 2013). Bilingual development differs from monolingual development in fundamental ways. Not enough is understood about this complex process. Accurate "norms" of bilingual development among different linguistic subgroups in the U.S. context are needed.

Classroom example: Consider the case of an emerging bilingual kindergartner, Lucas. His teachers are concerned about his lack of progress in early literacy skills and wonder if he may be "limited" in both English and Spanish. They administer the Peabody Picture Vocabulary Test in English (PPVT, Dunn & Dunn, 2007) and compare his performance with the norms provided in the test's manual. According to these norms, Lucas' score is below normal; in other words, his English vocabulary is limited in comparison with that of fluent English-speaking peers. Then they give Lucas a Spanish version of the test, the Test de Vocabulario en Imagenes Peabody (TVIP, Dunn, Padilla, Lugo, & Dunn, 1986). They find that his Spanish vocabulary is lower than that of fluent Spanish-speaking peers. They are confident that these two tests confirm their suspicion that Lucas has not had the opportunity to fully develop "language." Yet what if there is another way to think about this?

MacSwan (2000) challenged the widely accepted perception that many ELLs are "non-nons" (i.e., limited in both English and their native language). He asserted that such conclusions are due to faulty tests that have not been normed with similar emerging bilingual students and, thus, do not give us a sense for how well a child is progressing as someone who is developing multiple languages. What should be considered "normal" for a 5-year-old kindergartner who has grown up speaking some English and some Spanish?

Again considering Lucas: His score on the PPVT is 87; the mean for all students who took the test as part of the norming sample is 100. His score is below average to be sure, but by less than one standard deviation. In Spanish, his score is slightly lower, at 82. Again, that is below average. But what if we were to add the total number of words Lucas knows and compare his score in English *plus* Spanish with the scores of other emerging bilinguals? How would he compare? What if we also compared the total number of words he knows with the total scores of monolingual English speakers and also with monolingual Spanish speakers? It is very likely that he actually knows *more* words altogether. Shifting our thinking in this way can be quite illuminating. What if, rather than considering Lucas to be a child "at risk" because of his "non-non" or limited English proficiency, we think of him as a child with tremendous potential?

MacSwan (2000) also refuted *semilingualism,* insisting that ELLs come to school with language that is complex and fully evolved (see box, "Research-to-Practice Example"). He challenged the characterization of the language variation of ELLs in the United States in both English and their native language as being "low level," citing research by linguists who had noted that children acquire the language of their community by the age of 5 or 6 (Gleitman & Landau, 1994; Pinker, 1994). Studies on preschool language development indicate that when children begin school they already have "acquired most of the morphological and syntactic rules of their language" (Tager-Flusberg, 1997, p. 188). The reason ELLs can appear limited is that language assessments do not adequately measure the full range and depth of their combined linguistic skills in multiple languages.

MacSwan (2000) also argued that the underlying theory supporting the notion of "non-non" classifications is flawed. He attributed the focus on "non-non" classifications to the Cummins's (1979) conceptualization of semilingualism. Cummins described *semilingualism* as "low level[s] in both languages" (p. 230). Although Cummins (1981) substituted *limited bilingualism* for the term *semilingualism,* theoretically the two terms apply to the same concept (MacSwan, 2000). Limited bilingualism differs from what Cummins referred to as more advanced levels of bilingualism, *dominant bilingualism,* and *additive bilingualism* (i.e., native-like ability in one language and high levels in both languages). Cummins associated negative cognitive effects with limited bilingualism, neutral cognitive effects with dominant bilingualism, and positive cognitive effects with additive bilingualism.

MacSwan (2000) agreed with Cummins that language variation is real. However, he asserted that educators and others should not attribute language variation to differences in linguistic or cognitive ability. Blaming supposed lower levels of bilingual competence to negative cognitive ability results in social, academic, economic, and political disadvantages to ELL populations in the United States. MacSwan (2000) emphasized that "if teachers believe that some children have low language ability in both languages, then this belief may have a strong negative effect on their expectations for these children and the curricular content and teaching practices students receive" (p. 6). He stressed that this belief in semilingualism or limited bilingualism is so widely attributed to ELLs in the United States that it has become accepted as common sense. MacSwan noted that this deficit orientation ultimately sets in place a self-fulfilling prophecy for ELLs' academic underachievement.

Research-to-Practice-Example

MacSwan and Rolstad (2006) inspected the results of the Language Assessment Scales Oral—Español (LAS-E; De Avila & Duncan, 1990, 1994), the IDEA Proficiency Test I for Spanish (IPT; Amori & Dalton, 1996), and the Woodcock-Muñoz (WM; Woodcock & Muñoz-Sandoval, 1993), administered to 160 Spanish-speaking children, ages 6 to 8, who had recently scored "non" on the English version of the LAS-E (i.e., LAS-O). The research team elicited natural language samples from participants by asking them to tell a story in both Spanish and English while looking at a wordless picture book about a boy and a frog (Mayer, 1969). Then they coded the speech samples for lexical, morphological, and syntactic structures and errors. Next, they compared the results of the analysis of the natural language samples with the results on the formal native language assessments and found that the children scored at various levels of proficiency on the LAS-E, IPT, and WM, whereas they found little variation on the natural language samples in the rate of error in morphology and syntax in Spanish. The LAS-O, IPT, and WM identified large numbers of children as nonspeakers or as limited in their native language, but the Spanish language samples showed that all but two students showed no more than an 11% morphological error rate, with 94% of the students having an error rate of 5% or less. These children showed a mean morphological error rate well below the mean rate for normally developing children, as found by Reilly, Bates, and Marchman (1998). The error rate for one child was extremely high, suggesting possible language impairment. MacSwan and Rolstad (2006) concluded that the evidence from the natural language samples showed that the children in this study had learned the language of their community, even though many of them were identified as "non" speakers of their nativelanguage using standardized tests.

Adapted with permission from *Why Do English Language Learners Struggle With Reading? Distinguishing Language Acquisition From Learning Disabilities,* by J. K. Klingner, J. Hoover, and L. Baca. Copyright 2008 by Corwin Press

Misconception: Immersion in English Literacy Instruction Results in Faster Mastery

Isn't this just common sense? After all, research has shown that more time on task can increase academic outcomes. However, counterintuitive though it may be, a solid base in one's first language does more to help with English acquisition than submersion or immersion in an English-only environment. In fact, in their comprehensive review of research on teaching ELLs to read in English, August and Shanahan found that some native language instruction led to greater gains in English than no native language instruction (August & Shanahan, 2006). Other reviews have achieved similar findings (Genesee, Lindholm-Leary, Saunders, & Christian, 2006; Greene, 1997; Rolstad, Mahoney, & Glass, 2005; Slavin & Cheung, 2005). Goldenberg (2008) explained:

> The effects of primary language instruction are modest, but they are real and reliable. The average "effect size" is around .35-.40, depending upon whom is doing the calculation and how it is done (estimates range from about .2 to about .6). Translated, this means that primary language instruction can boost student achievement, in the second language, by about 12-15 percentile points. That's not huge but neither is it trivial. (¶ 7)

In other words, research supports teachers' use of their students' first language as a way to help them acquire English. Even when teachers do not speak the same languages as their students, they can still encourage strategic first language use. Doing so can help ELLs learn grade-level content while they are acquiring English, clarify misunderstandings, enhance vocabulary learning, and build a bridge to English. Use of home languages also helps to establish a bond between the home and the school. Skills students develop in one language transfer to English, and vice versa, particularly when the teacher makes these connections explicit.

An important reason that time on task in English is insufficient for helping students acquire English proficiency and learn to read is that instruction must be *comprehensible* (i.e., understandable) and at a suitable level to be helpful (Krashen, 1981). Krashen (1981) noted that ELLs acquire English as a new language by hearing or seeing messages that are slightly above their current level. He called this "Comprehensible Input +1." There are many ways that teachers can provide scaffolding to help ELLs make sense of the input, such as through gestures, visuals, diagrams, real objects, and/or simplified language.

Misconception: Errors Are Problematic and Should Be Avoided

It is common to misinterpret ELLs' errors in English as an indication they may have LD or perhaps a developmental delay (Harper & de Jong, 2004). Yet it is natural for students to overgeneralize new grammatical rules and to make errors while they are learning, just as young children do when learning to speak in a first language. For example an English-speaking 4-year-old might say, "I goed to the park." In fact, miscues indicate progress and are a sign that ELLs are feeling comfortable enough to take risks. Their mistakes provide clues about the ways they are drawing on their native language to help them learn a second language. This process is referred to as *interlanguage* and is unique to emerging bilingual students. It includes features of both languages. Interlanguage is characterized by confusion with verb tenses, plurals, possessives, subject/verb agreement, word order, and the use of articles (Ferris, 2002; Harper & de Jong, 2004). For example, *"el niño moreno tiene 7 años"* means "the brunette boy is 7 years old." However, a literal translation of each word would read, "The boy brunette has 7 years." A Spanish-speaking child who mistakenly says "the boy brunette" rather than "the brunette boy" or "he has 7 years" rather than "he is 7 years old" is transferring knowledge of Spanish to English. It is important to understand that this kind of confusion is a normal aspect of second language acquisition, not an indication the child may have a language disorder or disability. The features of interlanguage vary depending on the nature of the first language and the rules that govern it. For instance, students who speak Chinese as their first language will display a different interlanguage than those who speak Italian.

Interlanguage is different than *code switching,* which means to combine two languages or to go back and forth between two languages, interspersing one while using another. This is a common, natural phenomenon and should not be considered an error or sign of confusion (Genesee & Nicoladis, 2006). Code switching can be considered a sophisticated use of language for social purposes. It is used by speakers when they are each fluent in both languages.

Misconception: All ELLs Learn English in About the Same Way at About the Same Rate

What does it mean when an ELL seems slow to acquire English? How should we interpret that? Teachers know that students do not all learn in the same way, so it would seem obvious that ELLs would differ in their rate of learning English. We can all think of people we know who appear to learn a new language almost effortlessly, and others who exert great effort to learn a new language and still struggle, despite years of trying. Some people claim that acquiring a new language just comes naturally, although others lament the tediousness of the process. August and Hakuta (1997) noted in their summary of research on ELLs that "the most striking fact about second language learning, especially as compared with first language learning, is the variability in outcomes" (p. 37).

The language acquisition process varies so much for many reasons, including the striking differences in ELLs' background experiences, how much schooling they have already had (and in what languages), and how frequently they have opportunities to practice their new language (Portes & Rumbaut, 2001; Valdés, 2001). Cognitive ability can seem to have little to do with rate of second language acquisition, with some very successful, intelligent people learning another language quickly and others taking much longer. Whether a student is an extrovert or an introvert also matters, with extroverts more likely to look for opportunities to engage with others in conversation and introverts more likely to feel shy or self-conscious and avoid conversations.

An important factor that is sometimes overlooked is the relative status of the first language in comparison with that of the majority (target) language (Cummins, 2000). If ELLs believe their teachers and classmates do not value their language and culture or, even worse, that they disdain it, they may be less motivated to learn English as the dominant language of the society. They are more likely to respond to a teacher who is sensitive to and appreciative of their culture and language.

One reason for this misconception is that ELLs develop social language and can converse in English much more quickly than they can engage in cognitively demanding academic tasks in English. In the early stages, teachers tend to overestimate what their ELLs can cognitively do in English. Typically, it takes between 7 and 10 years for students to acquire full proficiency and actually be able to process in English, much longer than many teachers realize (Thomas & Collier, 2002). How long it takes varies depending on the nature of the instruction students receive as well as many other factors. Dual language programs appear to be the most effective for promoting true bilingualism.

Teachers should keep in mind that their ELLs may appear to be fully proficient in English before they are truly ready to engage in highly demanding, abstract tasks in English. Teachers and others may worry that their ELLs have LD because they are showing so little progress, or they will seem to know something one day and forget the next. Or they may misinterpret students' limited focus as a lack of motivation. With much frustration in her voice, one teacher shared, "These students tend to not understand what I say during instruction. *It seems like they are not listening"* (Orosco, 2010, p. 157). Yet the most plausible explanation for this behavior is that they are not as fully proficient in English as she thought.

Misconception: ELLs Can Only Engage in Higher Level Thinking After Mastering Basic Skills in English

If we think about it, we realize that this misconception cannot be true. And yet, we have been in countless classrooms where the ELLs were copying from the board or a book or filling out worksheets or drawing pictures or coloring rather than participating in activities with their classmates. It used to be that some researchers thought that emerging bilingual students acquire a new language in sequential order: first oral language, then literacy, and then writing. But what we now know is that the relationship between oral and written language is actually a reciprocal one. Reading and writing, even in kindergarten, can reinforce oral language learning. In other words, these different skills interact with one another. Learning to speak, read, and write at the same time leads to greater growth than oral language alone.

Escamilla and colleagues developed a comprehensive biliteracy program called Literacy Squared (Escamilla et al., 2010). Emerging bilingual students learn to talk, read, and write in two languages at the same time. Instruction in the two languages is different. In other words, this is not a program where students learn in English one day and then in Spanish the next as if the two languages were interchangeable. Rather, instruction builds on what students already know and can do. Every day, students participate in Spanish literacy and literacy-based English as a Second Language (ESL). The project's motto is "becoming bilingual better, not faster."

Misconception: Parents and Other Caregivers Should Speak English in the Home

As Nonie Lesaux of Harvard explains, the most important principle to keep in mind is that it is *language* that matters; lots of language. Whether it is Swahili, Spanish, or Arabic, students benefit from hearing, understanding, and talking—a lot. One reason this is so important is that it builds the background knowledge so important for making sense of text. We have often heard parents say that they were told by someone at their child's school to speak only in English at home, so that their children would learn English faster. The prevailing thought has been that hearing another language would confuse the child, and that the only important goal in the United States is to learn English. And yet it is clear that a second or even a third language does not confuse children; multilingual children around the world grow up speaking more than one language. Even infants can distinguish between different languages.

An important principle to understand is that developing a student's first language actually helps to facilitate development in the second language (Genesee, Geva, Dressler, & Kamil, 2006). No parent should feel that the way they communicate is "less than" or not good enough. Parents and other caregivers should be encouraged to speak to their children in their home language and engage with them in literacy-related activities in their first language, even when their children are being instructed in English in school (Wong Fillmore, 2000). We can help parents understand that the rich language in their homes is a gift. We want them to feel confident that they can help their children. Home literacy activities, such as reading aloud; telling stories; making lists; discussing television shows, movies, and the news; and reading environmental print (the print of everyday life; e.g. street signs, restaurant and store ads), should be encouraged for ELLs in their home language (Moses Guccione, 2012). Families are developing vital oral language and comprehension skills that students can transfer into English.

Standardized tests tend to underestimate ELLs' potential (Abedi, 2002; MacSwan, Rolstad, & Glass, 2002). For a classic example, consider the 2,100 students from the triethnic norming sample for the System of Multicultural Pluralistic Assessment (SOMPA;

Figueroa & Sassenrath, 1989; Valdés & Figueroa, 1994). The authors compared students' grade point averages, standardized reading scores, and standardized math scores in 1982 with their 1972 Full Scale Wechsler Intelligence Scale for Children (WISC-R; Wechsler, 1991) scores. They classified students who achieved at higher levels than predicted by their IQ scores as "overachievers," whereas students who achieved at lower levels than predicted were "underachievers." They found that Latino/a students who in 1972 had scored at or below the mean on the WISC-R were more likely than their Anglo counterparts to show above-expected school grades and achievement, thus placing them in the "overachiever" category (Klingner & Artiles, 2003). Among Latino/a subgroups, those students who spoke more Spanish in the home were most likely to be "overachievers," rather than students from mixed English/Spanish homes. Valdés and Figueroa concluded that decisions based on IQ can be quite inaccurate for some students, especially those who come from homes where Spanish is spoken.

In a more recent example, Hammer, Davison, Lawrence, and Miccio (2009) examined the changes in Spanish-speaking families' home language use over 3 years while their children attended preschool and kindergarten. They found that when families increased their use of English in the home, it did not help their children's English vocabulary or literacy development. However, it did slow down their Spanish vocabulary. Hammer et al. concluded that teachers should not request that parents change the language they use at home.

Conclusion

There is much about the second language acquisition process teachers should understand. Teachers who themselves have experienced learning a second language and who understand the structure of English as well as of other language systems are more likely to comprehend the ways in which students' errors reflect their attempts to communicate. When teachers can accurately interpret students' errors as clues about their language development and then provide encouragement and support, students benefit (Harper & de Jong, 2004).

- Which of these misconceptions struck you as one you have thought about? Jot down one or two of the misconceptions that got you thinking the most and offered an alternative way to consider an idea.

- Are you multilingual? Where and how did you learn another language? At home? In school? Traveling in another country? Was it fun? Think about how your experiences learning another language affected how you think about that language now.

- What was your reaction to the misconception about higher level thinking? Are you able to provide multiple entry points to every activity so that even students at beginning levels of English proficiency can be engaged?

CHAPTER 6

In What Ways Is Learning to Read in English as a Second or Additional Language Different Than Learning to Read in English as a First Language That Can Be Confusing for ELLs?

This chapter addresses:
- Similarities and differences in learning to read in a first language and second or additional language
- Multiple explanations for why students might lack phonological awareness
- How you can support your ELLs' vocabulary development

Have you ever been told that learning to read in English as a second or additional language is just like learning to read in one's first language? Perhaps you were even told that you can use the same tests, the same instructional methods, the same standards, and the same benchmarks with your ELLs as with your other students (Gersten et al., 2007). Although it certainly is true that there are many similarities between learning to read in English as one's first or a second language, there also are key differences (August & Shanahan, 2006). When the differences are downplayed, teachers and others might misunderstand why their ELLs are not progressing as rapidly as their English-speaking peers when taught with the same methods. They might mistakenly assume that they are not as capable. English language learners share common challenges when learning to read English as a second or additional language that can mirror the characteristics of LD (see Table 6.1).

Phonological Awareness

Phonological awareness tasks become much more challenging when a student's first language does not include the English phonemes addressed in the task. It is very difficult to distinguish auditorily between sounds not in one's first language or to pronounce them.

Table 6.1. Possible Problematic Aspects of Instruction for ELLs

Reading Components	Potential Challenges for ELLs
Phonological awareness	When the student's first language does not include some English phonemes: • The student is not accustomed to hearing these sounds. • It can be quite difficult to distinguish between sounds. • Pronouncing new sounds can be difficult. • Phonological tasks in general become more challenging.
Alphabetic principle	Some orthographies are very different than English; even when the orthography of the student's first language is similar to English, differences can be quite confusing. • Letters might look the same but represent different sounds. • Unfamiliar English sounds and their various spellings can make decoding and spelling difficult. • Not knowing the meanings of words limits the ELL reader's ability to use context clues. • Learning letters and sounds can seem very abstract.
Fluency	ELLs typically have fewer opportunities to read aloud in English and receive feedback than their English-speaking peers. • ELLs may read more slowly, with less understanding. • ELLs can have an accent and still read fluently.
Vocabulary	Students may become good word callers but not understand what they are reading. • ELLs can be confused by prepositions, pronouns, cohesion markers, words with multiple meanings, figurative language, and idioms. • False cognates can perplex students (e.g., *fast* in German means "almost"; *embarazada* in Spanish means "pregnant").

Table 6.1 *(continued)*

Reading Components	Potential Challenges for ELLs
Reading comprehension	Many factors affect comprehension, such as oral language proficiency, word recognition skills, fluency, vocabulary knowledge, ability to use comprehension strategies, variations in text structure, interest, and cultural differences. To determine what students comprehend, teachers should: • provide them with alternative ways to show understanding (e.g., in their native language, using diagrams), and • focus more on content than grammatical errors or accents.

Teachers, speech and language pathologists, and psychologists sometimes misinterpret why an ELL cannot hear the differences between sounds and erroneously conclude that the student has deficits in auditory discrimination or phonological awareness. Having an understanding of which English phonemes do not exist in the student's language can diminish the chances of making this error (see Table 2.2 and Kress, 2008, for lists of phonemes that do not exist in different languages). To more accurately assess the student's phonological awareness, use phonemes the student knows. Also, provide explicit instruction in unfamiliar English phonemes. In addition, keep in mind that the order of phonemes in a word matters. It is more difficult to distinguish and manipulate phonemes presented in an unfamiliar order.

Classroom Example: Maria teaches kindergarten ELLs. She knows that ELLs cannot develop phonological awareness in English until they are familiar with the sounds of English. So, Maria keeps in mind two aspects of phonological awareness: that students need to become familiar with the sounds in English; and that there are sounds that will cause confusion, which she needs to anticipate. She makes sure that her students have lots of experiences with fun and motivating songs, poems, chants, and read-alouds that allow them to hear and reproduce the sound patterns of English. Then, once she begins explicit instruction, she makes sure to provide more practice with sounds that can potentially cause confusion, either because they do not exist in the native language or because they are perceived as different in English but the same in the native language.

Alphabetic Principle

Similarly, ELLs may struggle with decoding, especially if their native language orthography is quite dissimilar from English orthography. Letters can look the same across languages but have very different sounds. For example, although most consonants in English and Spanish have similar sounds, vowel sounds differ. The short vowel sounds in English (/a/, /e/, /i/, /o/, /u/) are especially puzzling. For example, of these short vowel sounds, only one matches a Spanish vowel sound—and it is not the "right" one! The short /o/ sounds like /a/ in Spanish. If a Spanish-speaking ELL pronounces a vowel sound as he would in Spanish, the word sounds incorrect (e.g., saying *beet* instead of *bit*). The process of learning sound–symbol correspondence can seem abstract and confusing.

It is easier for us to learn and remember new information we can plug in or connect to existing schema. As a test of this idea, try this exercise: Have someone name 10 random words that have no apparent connection to one another. See how many you can remember. Then ask the person to name 10 words that are clearly related, such as different rooms in a house. Again, try to remember them. Which task was easier? Which way did you remember more words? Most likely you remembered more words the second way because it is easier to remember information we can readily connect. If you were trying to remember rooms in a house, you most likely visualized a house and perhaps even pictured yourself walking through different rooms. Consider what it would be like if someone asked you to do this same task in a week, without repeating any of the words. Would you remember any of the first set of words? How about the second set?

Also, ELLs are at a disadvantage when trying to figure out how to decode new words using context clues if they do not understand the meaning of the words. Teachers should look for ways to make instruction meaningful rather than abstract and to help students make connections between new learning and prior knowledge. We think of this as something to connect to or "hang one's hat on."

Fluency

Fluency is the ability to read quickly and accurately, with expression. Fluency requires both word recognition and comprehension. One challenge ELLs face is that they typically are provided with fewer opportunities to read aloud in English and receive feedback than their English-speaking peers (August & Shanahan, 2006). It is not uncommon for them to read more slowly and with less understanding than their fluent English classmates.

One way to help build fluency is to make sure students understand text and can decode all words before they read it. Opportunities to hear a more expert reader model fluent, expressive reading, such as through echo reading or partner reading, help. Struggling ELL readers might also listen to and follow along with books on tape or on CD (Hiebert, Pearson, Taylor, Richardson, & Paris 1998; Peregoy & Boyle, 2008). Antunez (2002) noted that fluency should not be confused with having an accent. Many ELLs and fully proficient English as a second language speakers read English with an accent, but they can still read fluently. When ELLs read more slowly and lack expression, teachers should recognize that this is quite common for ELLs and does not indicate a learning disability. At the same time, teachers should provide them with additional opportunities to practice oral reading.

Vocabulary

Vocabulary can present special challenges for ELLs, who are more likely to be confused by figurative language, common words such as pronouns and conjunctions, and words with multiple meanings. English language learners may be good word callers without understanding the meaning of what they are reading. It is important for teachers to differentiate between words that students understand in their native language for which they simply need English labels and words for which they do not understand the underlying concepts and would benefit from additional instruction. Explicit instruction with multiple opportunities for practice in meaningful contexts can help a lot.

Consider that your ELLs need help with more common words that can be confusing, such as prepositions (e.g., *on, in, above*), pronouns (e.g., *she* in the sentence, "Maria was not feeling well. She hoped she would be able to leave early."), and cohesion markers (e.g., *therefore, however*). Words with multiple meanings (e.g., *bat, light*), figurative language such as similes (e.g., "as quick as a cricket," "swims like a fish") or metaphors (e.g., "his stomach was a bottomless pit"), and idioms (e.g., "a piece of cake," "to know something inside out") can be especially challenging for ELLs. Many words in English have cognates in other languages (i.e., words that are the same or similar, such as *bandage*, which is the same in French and English, or *animal*, which is the same in Spanish and English). Knowing this can be quite helpful for ELLs who are already literate in their first language, especially when the teacher points them out.

Just because students have limited vocabularies, this does not mean they might have LD or lack intelligence. As a group, ELLs are every bit as intelligent as their fully English-proficient peers. Yet it seems to be human nature to assume otherwise. Astute teachers are aware of this and make sure they do all they can to help their students develop their vocabularies, while at the same time being careful not to judge their students as somehow less capable.

Reading Comprehension

Reading comprehension for ELLs is affected by many factors, including their oral language proficiency, ability to use comprehension strategies, knowledge of different text structures, interest, background knowledge about the topic of the reading, and cultural differences. Providing explicit instruction in comprehension strategies and text structures, building background knowledge, and helping ELLs connect with their prior knowledge all can help with comprehension.

English language learners often understand more of what they read in English than they are able to convey. Thus, providing them with alternative ways to demonstrate their understanding can help. Consider using diagrams (e.g., labeling the parts of a plant) or matching activities rather than essay exams. Also encourage students to respond in a combination of English and other languages, enabling them to draw from their full linguistic repertoire.

Contrasts in cultural understandings can make a difference (August & Shanahan, 2006). For example, the typical wedding ceremony is quite different across cultures. Thus, a student who is reading about a wedding in the United States but whose background knowledge is about weddings in India will have different expectations for what will happen in the text, and may become confused. In a study of this type, the readers from the United States understood more when reading about weddings in the United States, whereas the readers from India understood more when reading about weddings in India.

There are many promising practices teachers can use to help ELLs understand what they read and develop their reading comprehension skills (August & Shanahan, 2006). Teachers typically spend little time actually teaching reading comprehension strategies to their students (Durkin, 1979; Klingner et al., 2010). Rather, they are more likely to ask students comprehension questions about text they have listened to or read. Even though only a few students may raise their hands to answer (and probably not the ELLs), the teacher is likely to call on a student to respond, evaluate the student's response, and then move on (Cazden, 2001). The teacher might assume students understand better than they do, then later wonder why they did not do well on the test designed to assess their learning of the material.

On the other hand, teachers might think that their ELLs understand very little when in fact they comprehend a fair amount. English language learners may understand more than they can demonstrate orally or in writing in English. If they are allowed to show what they have learned using their native language or with alternatives to oral or written responses, such as through diagrams or demonstrations, oftentimes it becomes clear that they comprehend much more than was at first apparent. Teachers might also draw the wrong conclusions about ELLs' comprehension if they pay more attention to students' grammatical errors, their accents when speaking, or the mechanics of their writing, than they do to the substance of their responses. When the goal is to determine the extent to which students understand the material they are learning, the teacher's focus should be on the content rather than the form of students' answers.

Classroom example: Mario teaches seventh-grade science in a diverse, urban middle school. His state and school district have recently adopted the Common Core State Standards as well as a new curriculum that includes more reading. In the past, Mario did not use the set of textbooks provided to him. He reasoned that the books were too difficult for his students to access anyway, and so preferred to engage students in hands-on activities. Now his curriculum director, Sally, is mandating that all science teachers use their textbooks and make sure to provide students with ways to access and make sense of the text. He is flummoxed. He is sure the text is too hard for many of his students, and so he tells his director that he is "not a reading teacher."

Sally assures Mario that he will have assistance and invites him to 2 days of professional development on an instructional model the district is adopting, Collaborative strategic reading (CSR; Klingner, Vaughn, & Schumm, 1998, 2012). CSR is a research-based instructional model that has been successfully implemented and studied in culturally and linguistically diverse, inclusive classrooms from fourth grade through middle school (e.g., Klingner & Vaughn, 1999, 2000; Klingner, Vaughn, Argüelles, Hughes, & Ahwee, 2004; Klingner, et al., 1998; Vaughn et al., 2011). It was designed to be used with complex, expository texts. It includes strategies for getting the gist of a passage, asking and answering questions, monitoring comprehension, and taking steps to improve understanding and peer discussion. The structure of CSR is divided into before, during, and after reading activities. Once students have learned the CSR strategies from their teacher, they use them when working in small, collaborative student-facilitated learning groups.

At first Mario is skeptical. Yet when he observes students use CSR to figure out the meaning of unknown words, to come up with main idea (i.e., gist) statements, and to generate and answer their own questions about a science reading, he is impressed. His attention is drawn to the ELLs and how actively they participate. It occurs to him that this is not like the cooperative learning groups he remembers from school when it seemed as though one or two students did all of the work. In these CSR groups, everyone really is participating. There is a leader (who, as it turns out, is an ELL), a "clunk expert," a "gist expert," and a "question expert." Everyone writes their own information on individual learning logs and then they discuss in their groups what they have written. He never has been convinced that students can explain concepts to one another as well as he can. And yet he witnesses them helping each other quite effectively using "kid talk." He ponders about his own classes and students and thinks about who participates, who is quiet, and who disengages. He vows to pay more attention to participation structures in his class and to do more to find out what his students are capable of when provided with more support.

Conclusion

Misconceptions about ELLs abound. As you are considering your literacy instruction and how culturally and linguistically responsive you are, think about these questions:

1. Have I developed a strong, positive relationship with ELLs and their families?

2. Do I personalize instruction? Do I connect classroom learning to the student's daily experiences?

3. Do I value students' linguistic and cultural backgrounds and look for ways to show this?

4. Do I give enough attention to affect, interest, and motivation?

5. Do I pay sufficient attention to the development of oral language?

6. Am I aware of aspects of reading that can be confusing for ELLs?

7. Have I found out which sounds and letters are different in the student's first language than in English so that I can clarify misunderstandings and provide additional practice?

8. Do I adjust instruction to provide students with additional support when they do not seem to understand (e.g., explicit instruction at their level, more opportunities for meaningful practice)?

9. Do I preteach key vocabulary and use multimedia, real items, appealing photos, charts, and other visuals to help make instruction comprehensible?

10. Do I focus more on the content of students' responses than the form when checking for comprehension, and provide multiple and varied ways of demonstrating learning?

Focus Questions

- Were there any "aha" moments while you read this chapter? Explain.
- Select one difference in the way teachers highlighted in this chapter instructed their ELLs you would like to try. Explain.
- Which of the aspects of reading addressed in this chapter do you think is most important (in other words, most likely to lead to ELLs being misplaced in special education)? Why?

CHAPTER 7

How Can Schools Establish Structures to Facilitate the Process for Distinguishing Between Language Acquisition and Learning Disabilities?

This chapter addresses:
- The importance of collaborative teaming in decision making for ELLs
- Considerations for data teams and problem-solving teams
- Roles of key educators in the decision-making process for ELLs

In order to more accurately make the distinction between language acquisition and learning disabilities, it is necessary for schools and districts to have certain structures and processes in place for collaboration and effective decision making. The implementation of a multitiered instruction and assessment model such as response to intervention (RTI) facilitates a more equitable process of identifying struggling learners, especially when they are ELLs. We have learned valuable lessons from multitier models shown to be effective in reducing inappropriate referrals of ELLs to special education (VanDerHeyden, Witt, & Gilbertson, 2007) in addition to lessons learned from our own work with university-school partnerships. Essential to adequately making the distinction between language acquisition and learning disabilities within a multitiered framework are structures that incorporate collaborative teaming, data-driven and problem-solving processes, effective professional development, shared leadership, and clearly defined roles.

Collaborative Teaming

Collaborative structures in education—teachers working in collaborative groups—have been shown to have fewer referrals to special education than noncollaborative structures (Chalfant, 1989; Fuchs et al., 1990; Pugach & Johnson, 1995), especially for minority students (Gravois & Rosenfield, 2006). Historically, school teams have faced challenges in collecting and interpreting student information to make valid instructional and evaluative decisions for CLD students (Carrasquillo & Rodriguez, 1997; Figueroa & Newsome, 2006; Klingner & Harry, 2006; Wilkinson et al., 2006). Teams have often relied on anecdotal information rather than data, functioning from a deficit view where problems were considered internal to the child rather than the context; decisions were made with little regard to or misinterpretation of student language proficiency, and the team members interacted within a hierarchical decision-making structure that was often biased (Klingner & Harry, 2006). School teams must foster collaboration and shared leadership, include educators with expertise in working with bilingual students, and function from a framework that affirms students from diverse cultural backgrounds. According to Haager, Klingner, and Aceves (2009), the benefits of collaboration in a multitiered educational model include

- increased support for students,
- more options for intervention when working together,
- professional support for teachers,
- collaboration in lesson planning and assessment,
- flexibility to try new things one teacher could not do alone,
- increase in teaching methodologies, and
- another set of eyes to observe and help with problem solving.

In order to implement collaborative teams, educators should consider how different support teams can be structured to best fit the needs of their context given the personnel and resources at hand (e.g., RTI planning team, grade-level teams, data/assessment teams). The importance is that they are truly collaborative; have shared leadership; include educators with expertise in working with emerging bilinguals; include members who know how to interpret data for emerging bilinguals; include parents as valued partners, not as an afterthought; and function from frameworks with affirming views of emerging bilinguals. Although team members should create a problem-solving perspective, these students should not be thought of as "problems"; they are responsibilities of all involved. An essential question that teams ask is: What about the learning environment, curriculum, instruction, and the interaction among the students could be altered so that students will learn better? Schools that value shared leadership are able to utilize the expertise of the educators, specialists, and classroom teachers. They draw from people's strengths and are able to accomplish their goals more efficiently. From our experiences, it has been effective to have a person who leads a data team in addition to a school principal who is highly involved. It is also helpful if bilingual teachers, literacy specialists, master teachers, and special educators are involved in cluster team meetings and instructional decisions for all students, as they have valuable knowledge to offer. It is absolutely necessary that school teams include experts with knowledge about ELLs, second language acquisition, the interaction of language and learning, and how to interpret assessment data. Whether it is the tools that are utilized to collect data, or the language used in decision-making conversations, the message needs to reflect an affirmative view of bilingualism. Teams have to function from frameworks that consider students' native language as strengths to be built upon, not as problems that interfere with learning.

The Importance of Data Teams

In a system that is data driven, we are hearing more and more that teachers are overwhelmed with the amount of data collected—how to interpret the data to make instructional adjustments. It is essential to have systems in place for documentation of not only test data, but also intervention support, student background information, parent interviews, and classroom observations for all educators to reference. Electronic databases allow for educators to monitor progress, graph results, and communicate needs, especially if students are receiving intervention support from multiple specialists in multiple settings.

We have found that schools need to create space and time to look at data and problem solve instructional and assessment decisions based on data. This goes hand in hand with understanding whether ELLs have had adequate opportunity to learn. It is essential that classroom teachers are central to data teams and the data analysis process. Classroom teachers who become proficient in data analysis will be able to make effective instructional decisions for students on a daily basis. As this may be a new skill for teachers, it is helpful for schools to provide teachers with support in organizing, managing, and interpreting the plethora of student data that districts are collecting in addition to classroom data that may be collected more locally.

Data teams differ from more traditional problem-solving teams (PSTs; also known as student support teams, SSTs, or student intervention teams, SITs) yet can be effectively combined with PSTs to allow for increasing levels of support for students. Table 7.1 describes the differences between the two types of teams. Data teams focus on the classroom level of instruction in addition to the beginning levels of tiered interventions. Data teams also focus on classwide data sets and instructional adjustments based on the data. They problem solve for groups of students while, at the same time, flagging students they are seeing as not responding to culturally and linguistically responsive instruction. Problem-solving teams focus more on individual students who have already been placed in tiered intervention groups, who have perhaps gone through multiple rounds of interventions. They are the teams who help collect the student history, data from parents, and more comprehensive assessment data. Ideally, PSTs conduct classroom observations and tiered observations to ensure opportunity to learn.

Table 7.1. Differences Between Data Teams and Problem-Solving Teams

Data Teams	Problem-Solving Teams
Teams generally comprise 6 members Members include classroom teachers, principal, interventionists working with specific grade level, data support person, ESL teacher	Teams of 6–8 members Members include interventionists, parent or guardian, special education teachers, school psychologist, speech pathologist, social worker, principal, representative grade-level teachers, mentor teachers, ESL teacher
Team is subdivided into grade-level teams (elementary and secondary) and cluster teams (elementary)	Multidisciplinary team of specialists and generalists
Team meets 3 times a year (after universal screening measures) and weekly to plan and adjust instruction	Team meets weekly or bimonthly
Team: • Analyzes classroom data sets • Analyzes CBMs and language proficiency data • Identifies patterns in groups of student data • Uses data displays • Adjusts classroom instruction • Sets instructional goals • Decides on tier placements and movements • Selects strategies for classroom instruction and tier instruction • Selects plan for implementation • Selects timeline for progress monitoring • Alerts PST to students who are "nonresponders" to instruction and intervention	Team: • Analyzes class and individual data sets • Focuses on progress-monitoring tools • Performs gap analysis • Looks at rate of progress and growth models for ELLs • Considers "true" peers • Recommends adjustments of tiers and interventions • Considers appropriateness of instruction in Tier 1 • Conducts observations of classrooms and intervention instruction • Decides on referrals for comprehensive evaluation

Note. ESL = English as a second language; CBM = curriculum-based measurement; PST = problem-solving team.

Problem-Solving Teams

The RTI PST plays a key role in supporting teachers in Tier 1 and helping to improve instruction. Team members can offer support through analyzing data together, suggesting instructional adaptations, pointing teachers to resources for ELLs, or conducting peer observations with feedback. Teams can help teachers decide which students should receive Tier 2 interventions, implement Tier 2 or Tier 3 interventions, and help monitor and document student process. Perhaps one of the most important roles that PSTs play is determining which students should be evaluated for possible special education placement. The make-up of the team should be diverse and include members with expertise in culturally responsive instruction, English language acquisition, and bilingual education. The classroom teacher must be part of the team, and parents should be integral as well.

Taking a problem-solving approach that doesn't make the student the problem is essential. PSTs should function from a student-centered and data-centered lens, always thinking objectively about struggling students. Teams must continually discuss the quality of instruction in each tier, relying more heavily on data rather than anecdotal evidence. Problem-solving approaches require clearly defining the problem, designing a plan, implanting the plan, and evaluating the plan. This approach applies to not only the decisions for instruction and interventions, but also for analyzing data, interpreting assessments, and making decisions about referrals. The purpose of PSTs has shifted from a special education pre-evaluation to a true problem-solving model. Questions that PSTs commonly address include the following:

- With what exactly does this student struggle?
- What are the student's strengths on which we can build?
- What kind of instruction/interventions has this student already received and what were the results (both Tier 1 and Tier 2)?
- How can we support the teacher with some new ideas for Tier 1?
- How can we readjust the Tier 2 interventions?
- Are there other factors we can influence, such as motivation?
- How can we involve the family?

In addition to collaborative teams, schools need structures that ensure effective instructional alignment and progress monitoring for ELLs and meaningful professional development that allows for these practices to be sustainable. The scheduling of instructional interventions is a real issue in schools—especially if schools are implementing literacy in two languages or need to consider ELD support and/or special education services. Schools need to consider how to support the general education classroom teachers to not only provide effective core instruction, but also provide supplemental Tier 2 instruction in the general education classroom—providing the general education teacher with the skills to provide effective interventions for ELLs with or without specialist support. Additionally, teachers need support structures to communicate with specialists if Tier 2 support or ELD support is offered outside of the general education classroom. Teams need to establish a process for evaluating teacher effectiveness in implementing CLD instruction.

Roles and Responsibilities

What Are the Responsibilities of Principals?

The principal's involvement is essential in facilitating an equitable decision-making process for ELLs (see box, Principals Can Support). Principals should be helping to facilitate the development of a common vision, to incorporate data-based decision making into the current system, to provide tangible support for the process (e.g., staff time, budget allocations, intervention programs), and to ensure that staff remain on course (Ikeda et al., 2007). Of utmost importance is a school leader who promotes and fosters an affirmative view of bilingualism and an inclusive environment for CLD families. Principals are also advocates for their school community to seek out resources and form partnerships with other schools and universities.

Principals Can Support an Effective Decision-Making Process for ELLs by. . .

- Supporting teachers with instructional and assessment decision making.
- Selecting and modifying appropriate interventions for ELLs.
- Modifying instruction for ELLs.
- Supporting with data management.
- Supporting with interpreting data.
- Ensuring parents are valued as true partners.
- Observing and coaching teachers in classrooms and intervention groups.
- Modeling instructional practices.
- Creating resources for sharing of Tier 2 and Tier 3 interventions across schools.
- Partnering with other schools in district or universities for support.

What Are the Responsibilities of Classroom Teachers?

Classroom teachers are integral in ensuring the implementation of Tier 1 instruction that is culturally and linguistically responsive. Teachers need to document and demonstrate that this is integrated into their everyday practice and that they are able to adjust instruction based on progress-monitoring and universal screening data. Teachers have many insights to share with colleagues surrounding students' experiential background and learning needs in different contexts. Teachers must be able to analyze data and make instructional decisions based on data, and continue to develop their expertise on working with ELL students.

What Are the Responsibilities of Specialists?

Literacy specialists and interventionists provide knowledge and expertise that is essential to decision making for ELLs. They are able to identify specific areas where students may struggle with a concept and provide resources for targeted support. These experts should also be assisting with progress monitoring, data management and interpretation, and perhaps implementing supplemental instruction either in pull-out or push-in settings.

What Are the Responsibilities of ELL Teachers?

Educators with expertise in working with ELLs have a depth of knowledge about second language acquisition and the many factors that influence a student's learning. Not only may they be more familiar with interventions and instructional modifications that work well with ELLs, but they often know the students in a different context and can provide insight on students' language proficiency in all domains. Often, they are also more familiar with the families of ELLs and can act as an advocate ensuring the families' voices are heard and that communications are translated in student's home language.

Professional Development

The complex question of distinguishing language acquisition from learning disabilities continues to permeate our work. We have learned a great deal from research and practice, but there are still questions that remain unclear for all of us. We must continue to seek out professional development and have collaborative discussions around this important work. Professional development for educators needs to be ongoing and meaningful—perhaps moving away from more traditional presentation-based workshops to more problem-based small group sessions with educators sharing the responsibility of problem solving and learning together. Professional development also needs to address the beliefs of teachers and misconceptions about emerging bilingual students as well as the function of multitiered support systems, and explore a variety of topics (see box, Topics for Professional Development).

Topics for Professional Development

- Second language acquisition foundations.
- Common misconceptions of ELLs and how struggling ELLs might look like students with LD.
- Principles of RTI—how it differs from prereferral processes, historical development.
- Culturally responsive teaching.
- Intervention strategies—modeling/peer observations.
- Developing lab classrooms.
- Unit planning sessions to align CRT practices and language objectives with district curriculum/benchmarks.
- Book study groups with narratives about CLD families.
- Data team processes—developing tools and systems.
- Online learning modules for teachers to go through at their own pace.
- Video coaching with local university or master teachers.
- Creating home–community–school partnerships.

In our most recent work with school–university partnerships, we have focused on professional development that addresses the diverse needs and knowledge base of a teaching community. We draw from experts in the school who have worked with ELLs and have extensive knowledge about culturally and linguistically responsive instruction to create mentoring relationships with less experienced teachers. We have also created partnerships with other schools to maximize not only people resources, but also curricular and community resources for ELLs. During workshop sessions, we focus on creating a comfortable space for people to address real areas of need and real biases. Teachers work on activities that incorporate actual student data, problems, and potential solutions. Other ways for school leaders to foster effective professional development include teachers observing in other classrooms or schools, teachers videotaping successful practices to share with colleagues, or book study groups.

Classroom example: At Apple Valley Elementary School, the collaborative teams are designed to serve different purposes for meeting the needs of all learners. They have seen academic growth over the past 5 years and attribute a great deal of it to their collaborative structures. The principal is involved on all levels. The school has cluster team meetings, RTI problem-solving team meetings, and leadership teams meetings. The cluster teams are broken into two teams (K–Grade 2 and Grades 3–5). They include the principal, a data support person, all grade-level teachers, and any interventionists and

ELL teachers working with students at that grade level. The principal facilitates the meeting and has a clearly printed-out process they follow at each meeting. The cluster teams meet weekly to analyze student data, make instructional decisions, support each other with ideas for lesson planning, place students in intervention groups or change intervention groups, and consider progress-monitoring tools. Teachers utilize data that includes AIMSweb, DRA/EDL, WIDA-Access. Their data are stored electronically and easy to access. Teachers bring their laptop computers to work directly on the computer to look at data and document any changes. The principal assigned one person who is in charge of managing data: helping teachers stay organized and communicating between the district data person and the school. She helps track students moving in and out of intervention groups and helps monitor their progress with a data display posted in her office. The school's teaming is serving as a model for other schools in the district and starting to see referrals of ELLs decreasing.

Conclusion

There are essential structures and processes that enable an effective process, but schools may need to be creative in maximizing their resources. We acknowledge that insufficient school and district resources/supports are contributing factors that may limit the effective delivery of multilevel instruction and decision making for ELLs (Schwierjohn, 2011). Principals play an essential role in ensuring collaborative structures and shared goals for providing effective practice for ELLs. Levels of collaborative teaming that focus on problem solving, shared leadership, and data-based decision making are key to making effective and equitable decisions about ELLs.

Focus Questions

- What are some of the factors that facilitate or hinder effective collaboration at your school?
- How do the change agents (teachers, specialists) at your school define their roles?
- What are some of the ways your principal supports effective instruction of ELLs at your school? How do they foster collaboration?
- What types of professional development have you found to be effective?

CHAPTER 8

How Are Families Involved in the Process?

This chapter addresses:
- Parent's rights—what IDEA says
- Challenges and barriers to parent involvement
- Framework for involving families and parents
- Suggestions and solutions

Parents' Rights—What IDEA Says

It is important to include the families of ELLs as valued partners in their child's learning process. Families should be involved as early as possible and at multiple levels; they should be notified early when a child seems to be struggling and asked for their input. Federal law (i.e., Individuals With Disabilities Education Act, IDEA, 2006) specifies that families must be involved when a school is considering whether to conduct a comprehensive evaluation of a student. Families' rights of participation include

- The right to participate in meetings related to the evaluation, identification, and educational placement of the student.
- The right to participate in meetings related to the provision of a free appropriate public education.
- The right to be included in any meeting the purpose of which is to decide whether their child is a "child with a disability" and meets eligibility criteria for special education and related services.
- The right to be included on any team that makes placement decisions for their child or that develops, reviews, and revises an individualized education program for their child. Schools must make every effort to ensure their participation, including meeting individually or via conference calls.
- The right to consent to the school providing special education services.

In addition, schools must obtain written consent from parents or guardians to conduct an evaluation for special education. "Consent" does not mean that they are agreeing to special education if the child is found to be in need. All of the information provided to families must be presented in a language that they can understand (*Marple Newtown School District v. Rafael N.*, 2007).

Challenges and Barriers to Parent and Family Involvement

Research shows that parents from diverse backgrounds value formal schooling and academic achievement, want to help their children succeed, and are often able to do so, but schools often misperceive parents' expectations and fail to foster this relationship (Samway & McKeon, 2007, p. 61). Some common challenges to parent involvement include limited time to build trust, relationships, and ongoing two-way communication; limited skills and knowledge in how to partner; parents fear of inadequacy, conflict, or "reliving" negative experiences; cultural and linguistic differences between families and schools; and lack of clearly stated partnering beliefs, expectations of shared responsibility, and role descriptions (Esler, Godber, & Christenson, 2008). Each culture has its own perception of parent involvement in the schooling of children. What can appear to be a lack of value or disinterest in education by families of diverse cultures is often a difference of views of the roles of schools and teachers and the purpose of formal education (Valdés, 1996). Understanding families' views on education and their role in their child's education necessitates that often the school must reach out to parents. Jessica Martinez, Director of ELL Programs for Eagle County Schools in Colorado, is one school administrator with particular insight into the experience of ELL families; "turning the tables" by moving to an area where her own children were surrounded by others who did not speak the same native language highlighted for her the needs of ELL families in our schools (see box, Turning the Tables).

Turning the Tables

My husband and I have been trying to raise our children bilingually, but have struggled since our oldest child entered preschool. Speaking another language isn't really all that important when all of your friends speak English.

So this summer, I packed up my two children (ages 2 and just turned 5) and enrolled them in school in Mexico for the last month of the school year.

We did a lot of planning before we arrived. We researched the school and knew the language. I actually taught school in a neighboring city years ago, so we had an idea of what preschool was like in Mexico.

Turning the Tables *(continued)*

Imagine my surprise when I felt completely out of place. I did not realize that being a parent from another culture I would feel so lost.

I thought that this would be a great learning experience for my children, but it ended up being an incredible learning experience for me, as well. I got to see what school looks like through the eyes of a parent from a different culture.

Cultural Overload

I received a tour of the school the first day. But it was so different from what I know of as school, that I couldn't remember the details. I had too much information too fast and remembered almost nothing.

I couldn't remember what time lunch was. I couldn't remember what day was swimming class, so I just sent their swimming suits every day until I figured out a pattern. I had no idea what my girls were doing all day long. I would have loved to take home a booklet or have a link to a video on the school's web site that I could refer to again and again that would remind me of the basic necessary information I needed to know as a parent.

Forms

I had many forms to fill out so that the school would know more about my child. I was surprised that the teacher knew very little about my child after the first week of school. I realized that the forms were just requirements for the office and given to the homeroom teacher who may or may not read them.

I would have liked it if the forms would have been read by ALL of my daughters' teachers, including her English teacher and her Spanish teacher. There was information on those forms that would have saved time and helped the teachers meet my child's needs.

Communication

After a week, the cousin we were living with pointed out that all children in Mexico have homework. Even her toddler had homework once a week, but my girls had brought nothing home.

This was an incredibly stressful realization for me because I knew I had to go in and ask questions (and look stupid) in front of the teachers. They would find out that I didn't know what was going on in school and that I didn't even know the name of my child's teacher. I was so stressed out that I stayed up the night before to plan what I had to say.

We often see parents who are too nervous to come in and speak with the teacher. Many of the parents from other cultures may not come in to ask questions or address school issues. I can't imagine what it would feel like if I didn't speak the language.

Linguistically Diverse

When I spoke with the teachers, I discovered that because Sofia didn't know the language fluently, and she didn't automatically join in on the activities, the teacher thought she had no prior academic experiences. While the other students were practicing letter sounds, Sofia was given coloring sheets.

My child was the language learner in the back of the room, doing an easier activity, not receiving access to the curriculum.

If the teachers would have called me and let me know at the first sign they saw something wrong, they would have discovered that Sofia is actually an early reader in Spanish and she can write short sentences with invented spelling.

If they would have read the enrollment forms, they would have discovered that Sofia is distracted easily and that she will happily choose coloring over almost any other activity.

Turning the Tables *(continued)*

Because Sofia is a language learner, she looks like she is academically behind, even though she is actually ahead of the other children in her class.

This makes me think about all of the language learners in our schools who appear as "struggling learners." Are parents aware that we think their child is not on track? Is the child truly behind, or is it insufficient language, accommodations and lack of getting to know the student's academic level that causes the child to appear to have deficits, like in Sofia's case? Do parents find out in time, to help clarify or correct the issue?

If we partner with parents quicker, we might be able to solve issues right away. I can see that if my child is unable to participate in class for even a short period of time, she will fall further and further behind, eventually causing a gap in her learning. Imagine the effect of not being able to participate for weeks or months, as many of our newcomers experience.

Culturally Diverse

I don't know how to put little braids in my children's hair like the other girl's moms. We don't show up for school events, because I somehow didn't get the information. I put weird things in my kid's lunches, like a peanut butter and jelly sandwich. The teacher has to buy snacks for my kids at the school store, because where we come from, people don't send money to school with preschoolers. (I wonder if she thinks we can't afford it?)

As a parent from another culture, I hope the teachers look past the cultural and language differences and get to know my children for who they really are. I hope they realize that my children are smart and that they can achieve the same goals as anyone else. I hope they see my children's strengths and not just their language deficits. I hope they use strategies and provide ways for my children to access information and learn, rather than letting them fall further behind.

My children need different explanations to understand what is going on in school. They need extra supports in order to be able participate in class. They need more attention in order to be motivated.

Reprinted with permission from "How Do Newcomer Families Adjust to School?," by J. Martinez, in *Cultural Connections: Eagle Valley School District Newsletter,* 2013.

A Framework for Involving Families of ELLs

According to Epstein and Dauber (1991) the strongest and most consistent predictors of parent involvement at school and at home are the specific school programs and teacher practices that encourage parent involvement at school and guide parents in how to help their children at home. A common framework used by schools and districts to develop parent partnerships is Epstein's typology of six levels of parent involvement: parenting, communicating, volunteering, learning at home, decision making, and collaborating with the community (Epstein et al., 2009). These levels build upon each other and are a useful framework, however you must consider how parents and families of ELLs fit into this typology. Traditionally schools have taken the approach of educating parents and asking parents to conform to the culture and norms of the school, but approaching parent involvement as a partnership requires a "reciprocal understanding of schools and families" (Arias & Morillo-Campbell, 2008, p. 12). In other words, in addition to traditional models of family involvement that are culturally responsive, schools must implement programs and practices that incorporate and value the lived experiences of diverse families.

Parenting

One of the barriers to effective partnerships is the school's deficit view of families from diverse backgrounds. Parents of ELLs are sometimes seen as not having the language or resources needed to support their child's learning. One solution is for schools to offer family literacy programs where teachers and parents work together to agree upon effective ways to support their children at home. Schools can learn about how ELLs learn in their homes and communities and tailor educational activities to those experiences and parents can learn how to support their children in the U.S. education system. Schools can help create an environment where parents have a network of support (e.g., accessing community resources, seeking advice on parenting, taking English classes, or furthering their own education). One of the best ways to understand the families of your students and to begin a partnership is to conduct home visits. Even if there is a language barrier, extending that hand will communicate that you value their input.

Communicating

Common barriers for families of ELL students include lack of English proficiency, lack of knowledge of schooling practices, and different values about education. Communication that is consistent, organized, and systematic is essential to including parents in meaningful ways. Having access to interpreters and home communications in the native language is a must and a minimal requirement for communicating with families. Being open and explicit about how information will be communicated should be agreed upon among parents and educators to make the process function more smoothly. Strong communication systems and routines should be in place in Tier 1 before the child is even struggling so that there is already a basis from which to work. If a student is being considered for more intensive instructional support or more comprehensive assessment, educators need to be proactive in providing parents and families with information about the referral process, provisions of IDEA, and their rights—including what the individual state requires for RTI and disability determination. Families should be informed in writing that they can request evaluation at any time, and receive information about multitiered support systems such as RTI (e.g., addressing educational jargon, the essential components of each tier, the philosophy, processes). In addition, educators need to provide information to families about student needs and selected interventions (e.g., consider a written intervention plan). Progress should be reported regularly, and families should be involved during the planning of interventions. Educators and families can agree on opportunities to support children at home.

Volunteering

Parents of ELLs often want to be involved in the school setting, but may be discouraged by language barriers, unwelcoming school environments, or work schedules that conflict with the school day. Schools must communicate to families the various ways they can be involved and offer interpreters and translators and flexible schedules. One of the most effective ways to get them involved is to ask them through surveys how they can best offer their talents and skills to support the students. One example we have seen work well in elementary classrooms is having an "all about me" day for each student. They can invite their family in to become familiar with being in the school and have a bilingual teacher there for support. Another way to include families is to invite them to read a story to the class or present to the class on a topic of interest.

Learning at Home

One of the misperceptions about parents of ELLs is that they do not value education or they do not have time or skills to help their children be successful in school. Often ELL families are intimidated by not knowing *how* to help their children—not understanding the language or concepts being taught. Having an understanding of what literacy practices already exist in the home and valuing those experiences helps; teachers they can draw on those practices and incorporate them into learning experiences in the classroom as well as encourage parents to utilize those experiences to incorporate schooling practices in the home. Many families have a wealth of educational practices in the home that differ from traditional schooling experiences. For example, Reyes & Azuara's ethnographic study (2008) explored how specific language environments influenced the development of biliteracy in young Mexican Spanish–English bilingual children. They discovered that families demonstrated a wide variety of communicative practices and ways in which they participated in different literacy events at home (e.g., daily living routines, entertainment, literacy for literacy's sake, storybook time, interpersonal communication). They also found that adults and, often, siblings served as experts who scaffolded literacy knowledge as the young children progressed toward biliteracy.

A common misconception that both teachers and parents hold is that children must read or speak only in English in order to develop literacy and language skills in English. Encouraging parents to read to their children and speak to their children in their native or first language can provide a foundation for transferring academic skills, concepts, and meta-language abilities to be successful in second-language acquisition. Including parents in meetings where teachers develop goals and interventions for students will allow parents a better understanding of how to help their children at home.

Decision Making

Studies of child support teams have noted that parents' voices are often the least heard among the members present at the table (e.g., Klingner & Harry, 2006). In a truly shared partnership, school teams will find meaningful ways to encourage parent voices (see box, Guidelines for Including).

Guidelines for Including Families on School Teams...

- Accommodate parents' schedules when considering meeting times.
- During the meeting, make sure all team members are introduced and their roles explained, clearly state the purpose of the meeting, and ask parents if they agree or disagree when members make decisions or offer solutions.
- Ensure they understand the acronyms and educational jargon being discussed, and that they understand the purpose and types of assessment data and academic benchmark goals.
- Make sure documents are translated in writing or interpreted orally. If an interpreter is present, talk directly to the parent, not the interpreter.
- Ask parents what they are seeing at home as far as behavior, language spoken, homework tasks, and so on; ask them if they have any specific concerns. Find out about the student's educational history and interests.
- Be sure to emphasize the student's strengths; it can be overwhelming to hear a lot of concerns at one time.
- Ask for input when designing interventions.
- Agree upon the best way to communicate with the family and establish who will follow through.

Collaborating With the Community

Schools that have ties with the community can provide a more holistic educational experience that bridges the many contexts of a student's life. For ELL families, schools can partner with communities to offer ESL classes or family literacy nights. Educators can invite communities into the schools to bring "funds of knowledge" (Moll et al., 1992) into the curriculum. Schools with established school–community connections often have more services to offer ELL students and this is something to consider when a student is struggling in school—whether or not a student has access to a lot of resources (e.g., after-school tutoring, mobile library, summer literacy programs, technology business grants). The Colorado Department of Education developed a list of suggestions for ways schools can reach out to and include families of ELLs in their community (see box, Thinking About Solutions).

"Thinking About Solutions": Ways to Include ELL Families in the School Community

- Hold meetings for immigrant parents to explain how parent involvement is carried out in U.S. schools. Topics for such meetings may include how to access student grades and attendance online, explanation of high school credits and graduation requirements, and methods for supporting literacy in the home.
- Encourage parents to continue using their home language in the home and read to their children in their own language.
- Provide translators who can also act as cultural brokers for parent meetings and school events so parents feel more comfortable asking questions.
- To be more accessible, have staff come in early or stay late once a week.
- Share beliefs and expectations with families as equal partners with shared responsibility regarding student homework, behavior, and so on.
- Communicate creatively: Consider means such as texting, e-mailing, listservs copied to students, voice mailing, web sites, breakfasts, lunches, and meeting at school day-care centers.
- Pursue joint "professional development" where families, educators, and community resources learn together; investigate online opportunities.
- Host small gatherings with families and students; have class "open houses" at various times, drop-in centers.
- Explore ways for families to participate in and provide feedback on homework.
- Appoint "student ambassadors" who undertake home and school communication tasks, teaching parents, calling families to invite them to school.
- Identify cultural and language liaisons; family to family, home and community visits.

Note. Adapted from *Family & Community Partnering: "On the Team and at the Table,"* Colorado Department of Education, 2009.

One recent study offered some guiding principles for collaborating with culturally and linguistically diverse families. Blue-Banning, Summers, Frankland, Nelson, and Beegle (2004) interviewed 137 families from culturally and linguistically diverse backgrounds about collaboration and identified six characteristics of effective collaboration:

- Communication that is positive, understanding, and respectful
- Commitment to the child and family
- Equal power in decision making
- Competence in implementing and achieving goals
- Mutual trust
- Mutual respect

Blue-Banning and colleagues suggested schools develop a progressive plan to develop such collaborative relationships that include parents in the collaborative relationship from beginning to end, help teachers better understand the needs of families from culturally diverse backgrounds, and include activities designed to strengthen the trust that culturally diverse parents hold for educational professionals in the IEP process.

Classroom example: Parents have a wealth of knowledge about their child's strengths and struggles—if we only ask. A few years ago, a child study team was considering whether to evaluate a second-grade student for special education. The team consisted of the parent, an interpreter, a special education teacher, a speech–language pathologist, a social worker, the principal, the classroom teacher, and the ELL teacher. The educators had concerns about the language and literacy progress of the student. They had met about the student every year starting in kindergarten. In addition to reviewing the student's academic progress, the speech pathologist had concerns about the second-grader's ability to produce consonant clusters. When speaking with the child's mother, she found out that this was happening in Spanish as well: He was mixing up specific letters and sound combinations in both languages. The mother was also concerned that he had started speaking later than her other children in Spanish and suspected a possible language delay that might have affected him. The team decided to pursue further evaluations after speaking with the mother and looking at the body of evidence. After the meeting, the team expressed that they wished they had talked to the mother sooner.

Conclusion

Involving families as true partners in their child's education is an essential piece to understanding student learning and making effective decisions for ELLs. Families should be valued partners in any decision-making process from the very earliest stages. IDEA outlines parents' rights in the special education process, and it is important for all educators to understand these rights. Schools have encountered many barriers to involving families, especially families of ELLs, but there are many ways to facilitate genuine partnerships by approaching family partnerships with a comprehensive framework.

Focus Questions

- What strategies has your school implemented to form family school partnerships?

- What are some of the barriers to family partnerships that have impacted the families of your ELL students? Write down some solutions.

- How do your decision-making teams involve families of ELLs as equal partners?

- What is one take away from the chapter that will affect how you interact with parents of your ELLs this year?

CHAPTER 9

How Can We Tell Which ELLs Should Be Referred for a Comprehensive Evaluation?

> This chapter addresses:
> - Steps to take when deciding whether to refer an ELL student for consideration of special education eligibility
> - Data analysis and the importance of comparing ELL students to "true peers"
> - Distinguishing between responders and nonresponders

In this chapter, we discuss the natural progression of steps that will help you decide whether an ELL warrants an official referral for special education evaluation. As a rule, you should be taking the approach that the student's struggles may be caused by external factors rather than internal factors and maintain this hypothesis until the data suggest otherwise. You must ensure appropriate referrals of ELLs at your school because "most students referred for consideration of special education are eventually placed in special education programs" (Hosp & Reschly, 2003, p. 10).

ELL Response to Schoolwide Instructional Approach (Tier 1) and Interventions (Tiers 2 and 3)

To determine which ELLs to refer for an evaluation, a useful rule of thumb is to look at how many ELLs are struggling in a class or across classes at a particular grade level. If the majority of ELLs are making little progress, then the focus should be on improving instruction and making sure it is appropriate for ELLs. By looking at class sets of data you can determine if there are patterns across groups of student learning or if a few students are struggling due to other factors. If most ELLs are doing well and only a few are struggling, it is suitable to look more closely at what is going on with those individual students and consider that they may have a disability. The first step is to observe the classroom.

When observing in classrooms, you should ask the following questions:

- Is instruction targeted to and appropriate for the student's level of English proficiency and learning needs?
- Is ELL instruction of high quality?
- Does the classroom environment seem conducive to learning?
- Are most of the student's true peers succeeding?
- Is the student's cultural and linguistic background taken into consideration when planning instruction?
- Does the classroom provide opportunities for students to interact and to use language and engage in meaningful ways?

Most of these questions can be addressed by teachers' and school teams' regular classroom observations and grade-level teams' regular procedures for analyzing data. School districts and researchers who have been implementing multitiered instruction models for many years have developed tools for analyzing data and making data-informed decisions as a foundation for tiered instruction (Kovalski & Pederson, 2008). Figure 9.1 provides an example of a document that captures classwide data analysis. This tool groups students by their proficiency on designated benchmarks and grade-level goals. Students are grouped along a continuum to see which students need the most intensive support and compared to what previous goals were or were not met. This type of analysis also allows for documentation of specific instructional strategies and adjustments with direct links to data and evidence.

When you are organizing class sets of data and considering academic benchmarks, you must specifically consider your ELLs and how they are developing as a subgroup in your classroom, not only with benchmarks but also with their language proficiency. Questions to consider include:

- How many ELLs do I have in my class?
- What are their proficiency levels for each language domain (i.e., speaking, listening, reading, writing)?
- Is there a disproportionate number of ELLs identified as "at risk"?
- With which items did ELLs struggle with most?
- Which, if any, modifications have been made to support ELLs? Do any modifications reflect "best practices" for ELLs (see, e.g., Gersten & Baker, 2000; Samway & McKeon, 2007)?

Figure 9.1. Analyzing Classwide Student Data

Classwide Student Data

Data content area (check one):

___ Oral reading fluency

___ Vocabulary

___ Oral reading comp

___ Silent reading comp

___ Word analysis

Student Names	Need More Time	Close to Proficient	Proficient	Above Proficient

Student Totals	ELL	Non-ELL
Percentage of students who need more time		
Percentage of students close to proficient		
Percentage of students at proficient		
Percentage of students above proficient		

Observe ELLs in All Instructional Contexts

Teachers and school leaders must consider how they will incorporate systematic observations of core instructional settings as well as tiered intervention settings. It cannot be simply assumed that all teachers are implementing culturally and linguistically responsive practices and effective practices for ELLs. Some schools integrate observations of instructional contexts into their teacher development or evaluation programming and designate specific items toward meeting the needs of ELLs. Other schools establish a separate observation once a student is beginning to struggle in the classroom. Either of these procedures can and should be used as documentation of adequate opportunity to learn.

In our observations of RTI team meetings, we have noticed that when considering an ELL, teams often discuss the quality of Tier 1 instruction, but only anecdotally. For example, they say, "Well, he is in Mr. Sanchez's class, so he hasn't had much language support." This can lead to a biased view of what actual instruction is happening in the classroom and does not provide much evidence to work with. We have been surprised at how many of these types of statements dominate the conversation. It is also surprising how many ELLs are referred for comprehensive special education evaluations without ever being observed in the classroom or in their intervention groups—which are often taught by teacher aides who do not have any training in working with ELLs. Especially when working with packaged intervention programs, it is essential to know how to meet the need of ELLs. Formal observations can help clarify potential misunderstandings and biases and prevent inappropriate referrals.

Once it is confirmed that most ELLs in a classroom are thriving and you still have concerns about a student, the next step is to collect individual student data. Individual student data should consider the student's strengths as well as struggles across all contexts and instructional settings. The following questions must be considered:

- Is consideration given to the child's cultural, linguistic, socioeconomic, and experiential background?
- Are multiple assessments used?
- What tasks can the student perform and in what contexts?
- Does the student differ from true peers in rate and level of learning?
- Are the child's parents involved as valued partners? What is their perspective?
- Does the data consider the learning trajectory of a simultaneous bilingual student?
- What is the student's educational history? Are there any gaps?

When comparing ELLs to other students, they must be compared to their true peers—not only students with similar cultural backgrounds, but students who share similar educational experiences and similar language proficiency levels (Brown & Doolittle, 2008). When grouping students by language proficiency, consider the domains of language and not just the students' oral language proficiency or overall scores. It might be more productive to consider their true peers based on students' reading or writing proficiency levels in addition to their educational and home experiences.

Providing Effective Intervention Support for ELLs

Teachers need knowledge of when and how to adapt interventions for ELLs. Educators should ask the following: If the student is not responding to the intervention, did it need to be adapted, or sustained? Do students have opportunities to apply skills of intervention in meaningful ways? Was instruction provided in isolation without opportunities to practice and receive feedback (Fisher & Frey, 2010)? Table 9.1 suggests levels of response when considering an individual student's response to intervention (Martinez & Batsche, 2008).

Table 9.1. Levels of Response to Intervention

Student Response	Levels of Response
Positive response	Gap is closing Can extrapolate point at which target student will "come in range" of target—even if this is long range
Questionable response	Rate at which gap is widening slows considerably, but gap is still widening Gap stops widening but closure does not occur
Poor response	Gap continues to widen with no change in rate

Tier 2 and 3 interventions must be in addition to or supplemental to and aligned with Tier 1 core instruction. Interventions may incorporate a different curriculum than Tier 1, but instruction must be systematic and explicit with modeling and feedback. All instruction should be culturally and linguistically responsive, use approaches that have been shown to be effective for ELLs, and incorporate oral language development. If a student continues to struggle even with supplemental Tier 2 and Tier 3 supports, there are some guiding questions to ask (Brown & Doolittle, 2008):

- How many rounds of supplemental instruction has the student received?
- Is there evidence of progress from previous interventions?
- Is the student successful with different curriculum, teaching approaches, and an individualized setting?

- Does the student differ from like true peers in level of performance or learning slope?
- Has the student received continuous instruction (e.g., consider absences and changes in schooling environments)?

Distinguishing Between Responders and Nonresponders

One of the pervasive questions in implementing a multitiered model of support to identify students with potential learning disabilities is how to know when students should be evaluated for special education or when they need more or different intervention support. Essentially, how do we identify nonresponders (students who are not responding to instruction and intervention)? This is a problem that is still being researched, but we do have some promising guidelines to work with. Research has shown that ELLs provided with high-quality interventions respond to those interventions to the extent that they may no longer be considered at risk (Linan-Thompson et al., 2006; O'Connor, Bocian, Beebe-Frankenberger, & Linklater, 2010). Research also indicates that responsiveness to instruction and intervention is related to teacher effectiveness across the tiers, the educator's ability to adapt and change instruction for nonresponders, and fidelity of implementation of high-quality instruction for ELLs (O'Connor & Klingner, 2010). Once we ensure these qualities are met, then we can consider some emerging characteristics of nonresponders:

- Does the student continue to display characteristics of summer loss?
- Does the student demonstrate poor phonological awareness and sometimes poor rapid naming, attention, or spelling? (Nelson, Benner, & Gonzalez, 2003)
- Does the student demonstrate problem behavior, poor knowledge of the alphabetic principle, or poor memory? (Al Otaiba & Fuchs, 2002)

Research is inconclusive about what level and rate of student response are sufficient to ensure the likelihood that a student will progress after Tier 2 support is discontinued (O'Connor & Klingner, 2010). Some students respond well to intervention for lower-level reading skills but begin to struggle when reading tasks become more complex. Some students may not have LD but require Tier 2 support to continue to thrive academically. Many good responders need the additional support provided by Tier 2 instruction to maintain steady growth.

Determining decision rules for interpreting progress-monitoring and other assessment data is often left up to the school district. Currently there is no real consensus on which measures most accurately determine response to instruction and intervention for ELLs. Districts and school teams must decide on the process they are going to follow and provide teachers with opportunities to accurately interpret data.

The following measures are recommended for determining adequate progress for ELLs:

- *Cut score:* Minimum proficiency level score below which learner is considered at risk or struggling (e.g., 25%).

- *Rate of progress:* Rate at which learner should progress to maintain acceptable progress.

- *Gap/discrepancy analysis:* Difference between expected and actual proficiency levels/progress rate.

Rate of progress needs to be considered in relation to true peers in addition to monolingual learners. In addition, it has been established that many struggling ELL readers can achieve at least average levels of performance when provided with supplemental, high-quality interventions during early stages of reading development (Lesaux & Siegel, 2003; Vaughn et al., 2006a, 2006b).

Conclusion

Determining whether an ELL should be referred for a more comprehensive evaluation should follow a series of steps to ensure an accurate process. First and foremost, you must confirm that a student has been engaged in high-quality instruction based on evidence from observations and data analysis. This includes ensuring intervention support is also high quality for ELLs and linked to core instruction. Although researchers are still seeking to establish the parameters for distinguishing responders and nonresponders, we do have some promising guidelines to live by. It is important to remember you are systematically ruling out all other contextual factors before considering whether a student has learning disability.

Focus Questions

- How well do your school teams utilize class sets of data to adjust instruction for ELLs during core instruction/Tier 1?

- How well do your tiered interventions incorporate effective instruction for ELLs and develop both language skills and content knowledge? List the strategies that are used.

- What decision rules does your school or district have in place to determine responders and nonresponders?

CHAPTER 10

What Does It Mean to Use an Ecological Framework to Determine Whether ELLs Have LD?

> This chapter addresses:
> - The definition of an ecological framework for ELLs
> - Types of assessments and their purposes in distinguishing language acquisition and LD
> - Considerations for assessing ELLs

In the field of special education, the long-time use of a discrepancy model for identifying students with LD fostered a deficit approach to learning. The discrepancy model focused attention on a student's inability to succeed in the general education classroom without considering the many environmental factors that have a major influence on academic or behavioral success. Some educators might have felt that an LD classification would at least get their students the support they needed outside of the general education classroom. However, problems associated with inappropriate classification and placement based on this model include being denied access to the general education curriculum, being placed in separate programs with more limited curriculum, and being stigmatized.

A shift toward a more comprehensive, ecological approach ensures a more equitable process of identifying students who truly have special education needs—and this includes ELLs. An *ecological framework* (Bronfenbrenner, 1979) considers contextual factors that can affect a student's performance as well as intrinsic factors. Such a framework for evaluating ELLs should have four elements:

1. A systematic process for examining the specific background variables or ecologies of ELLs (e.g., first and second language proficiency, educational history, socioeconomic status, cultural variables).

2. Information gathered through a variety of informal and formal assessments.

3. Examination of the appropriateness of classroom instruction and the classroom context based on knowledge of individual student factors (see discussion in Chapter 4).

4. Nondiscriminatory interpretation of all assessment data.

Bronfrenbrenner's ecological model (1979), when applied to education settings, has four environmental systems that capture the contextual factors that may influence a child's development. The **microsystem** includes the relationships that a child experiences in individual settings (e.g., home, church, store). The **mesosystem** includes the integration of experiences within individual microsystems (e.g., relationships between home, community, and school settings). The **exosystem** includes settings associated with other individuals significant to the student's life. Finally, the **macrosystem** integrates the previous three systems.

Table 10.1. Ecological Framework for Educating ELLs

Ecological Factors	Data-Gathering Practices
Learner characteristics	
Language proficiency	Analytic teaching, running records, language samples, language assessments
Experiential/educational background	Parent/student interviews, review of records, work samples
Classroom characteristics	
Challenging curriculum	Classroom observations, unit analyses, work samples
Culturally responsive instruction	Classroom observations, unit analyses, work samples
Home–community characteristics	
Home language(s)	Home language survey, parent/student interviews, review of records, home visit
Family educational history	Home language survey, parent/student interviews, review of records, home visit

Note. Adapted with permission from *Differentiating Learning Differences From Disabilities: Meeting Diverse Needs Through Multi-Tiered Response to Intervention,* by J. Hoover (p. 109). Copyright 2008 by Pearson.

This framework allows us to consider the multiple influences on a student's academic success. It is important to consider the unique characteristics ELLs bring to the learning environment within this framework. Think about how their familiarity with and exposure to English, socioeconomic status, prior schooling experiences, and life experiences interact with learning. Learner characteristics that need to be considered include language proficiency in English and home languages, acculturation, experiential background, values or norms, higher order thinking skills, and individual learning style. Classroom characteristics include language of instruction, functional use of language, instructional conversations, and challenging curriculum. Home–community characteristics include: home language, adjustment to new environment, socioeconomic status, and family educational history. Table 10.1 describes an ecological framework for educating ELLs and suggested practices for gathering data in each category (Hoover, 2008).

Comprehensive Assessment and Nonbiased Interpretation of Data

There is no single test educators can use to distinguish learning disabilities from language acquisition. The main issues to consider when using an RTI assessment system for decision making for ELLs are

- the importance of using multiple measures (both formal and informal),
- the different purposes of assessment in an RTI framework, and
- nonbiased interpretation of assessment information for ELLs (understanding what is different).

Using multiple measures to make educational decisions for ELLs ensures more accurate identification of individual students' strengths and needs; most standardized testing procedures are not sensitive enough to the unique educational needs of ELLs. Educators should utilize a combination of measures to provide a more comprehensive measure of ELLs' language and learning potential across educational contexts and specific to the real-world learning environment. Some measures that have been shown to be particularly effective for ELLs include curriculum-based measures, dynamic assessment framework, and performance-based measures.

Curriculum-based assessment (CBA) is an evidence-based strategy for measuring both level and growth in student performance (Linan-Thompson et al., 2003). Curriculum-based measures (CBMs) allow for multiple, ongoing, brief assessments that provide frequent data points informing response to instruction. Common CBMs used by school districts include AIMSweb (Shinn & Shinn, 2003), DIBELs (Good & Kaminski, 2002), or IDEL (Baker & Good, 2006); these CBMs can provide valuable assessment and instructional information. The use of CBMs as part of a comprehensive assessment approach has many benefits for ELLs. CBMs enable frequent monitoring of progress toward benchmarks in a systematic way. They can be used to measure students' response to intervention by being implemented frequently and they can be used to inform classroom instruction (Fuchs & Fuchs, 1997). Classroom teachers can use CBMs to determine if all ELLs are meeting goals in the classroom, if they need to adjust their instruction, and to determine which ELLs' needs supplemental support. Some CBMs offer assessments in Spanish and English for native Spanish speakers, and CBMs allow educators to consider ELLs' rate of progress in both L1 and L2 (De Ramirez & Shapiro, 2006).

Dynamic assessments allow educators to observe a student's responsiveness to instruction or intervention by measuring learning potential rather than previous experiences or learning. Using a test-teach-retest procedure, the educator can remove or incorporate learning support to mediate the learning process and assess student's use of learning strategies (Spinelli, 2008). For example, in retelling a story about a picture book, the teacher may be looking for elements of story structure and language proficiency. The teacher focuses on areas of difficulty and then has the student retell the story; this allows the teacher to assess the student's ability to modify the story and apply the support structures independently. This type of diagnostic assessment has been shown to provide information about students with suspected learning disabilities (Moore-Brown, Huerta, Uranga-Hernandez, & Pena, 2006).

Performance-based assessments are based on students' demonstration of learning through authentic products (Bender, 2002). These assessments have students construct a response or perform a demonstration, and then they are evaluated based on established criteria. These types of assessments have been known to promote higher level thinking abilities, integrate different skills and concepts across content areas, and demonstrate the learning process and product simultaneously. Examples of performance-based assessments include role-playing a story retelling, using graphic organizers to compare and contrast story elements, graphing the effects of water and sun on plant growth, or building a mathematical model. Performance-based assessments allow ELLs to demonstrate their abilities based on their level of language proficiency and personal experiences. Educators can track student progress through portfolios and rubrics that demonstrate growth and move toward benchmark learning targets.

When administering an assessment as part of a comprehension evaluation, a few questions can help guide the process:

- What do I want to find out?

- What can I learn from this assessment (i.e., what is its purpose)?

- What will I do with the information?

- What other explanations might there be for a student's performance?

Assessments used in an RTI framework serve different purposes; understanding those purposes can help educators avoid misinterpreting assessment data. Three primary purposes include screening, progress monitoring, and diagnostic. *Screening measures* help identify students at risk for learning disabilities. Most screening measures occur three times per year and school teams meet to discuss screening data at each grade level. Screening measures evaluate the effectiveness of the core curriculum in addition to identifying struggling learners early in the year. *Progress monitoring* occurs more frequently depending on the level of instruction. Some skills and concepts being taught need to be measured weekly, some only monthly. These more frequent measures allow educators to assess the link between what is being taught and student's response to instruction or intervention. *Diagnostic assessments* are more targeted and more often used for placement decisions in Tier 3 instruction or for special education services.

A Team Approach to Assessment for ELLs

When assessing ELLs (Lesaux & Marietta, 2012; see box, Some Considerations), it is helpful if school teams have a system for collecting, organizing, and interpreting assessment data and include the professionals with expertise in working with ELLs. Teachers are on the front line and have the most interaction with students in multiple contexts and learning situations. Teachers and school teams should take an additive approach and consider what strengths the student brings to the learning environment. As part of this process, English language acquisition specialists should assess ELLs' language proficiency and academic skills in English and the first language (using language samples, running records, and/or formal assessments). Special education teachers, psychologists, and/or speech language therapists may conduct additional formal and informal assessments based on their expertise. Teams can gather student background information through family interviews, review of records, portfolio assessments, and home visits. Higher order thinking abilities, learning styles, and various classroom characteristics can be assessed though curriculum-based measures, classroom observations, performance-based assessments, or reciprocal teaching. Professionals must continuously consider these factors to accurately determine tiers of instruction, actual interventions, and whether to consider a referral to special education. It is often forgotten that team members should observe the child in different contexts to better understand the instructional environment and under what conditions the student seems to thrive or struggle. This observational data is essential to understanding the bigger picture.

Some Considerations for Assessing ELLs

- Early literacy screening batteries often focus on print awareness, phonological awareness, and letter-word identification; they often do not include measures of vocabulary knowledge, oral language proficiency, or listening and reading comprehension.

- In the domain of vocabulary, as is the case with many native speakers, linguistically diverse students often have receptive vocabularies that are much larger than their expressive (or productive) vocabularies.

- An ELL student might have a broad, but not very deep, vocabulary, such as only having one meaning (the common one) for words with multiple meanings.

- Second language acquisition is an uneven developmental process. Some skills might develop more quickly than others; for example, some linguistically diverse students with good vocabulary knowledge might still have difficulty with grammar. (Lesaux & Marietta, 2012)

Focus Questions

- How does your school take an ecological approach to determining LD?
- How do you collect background data on ELLs?
- What forms of assessment are collected for ELLs at your school?
- Are there informal assessments you haven't considered that could provide useful information for your ELLs?

References

Abedi, J. (2002). Standardized achievement tests and English language learners: Psychometric issues. *Educational Assessment, 8*(3), 231-257. http://dx.doi.org/10.1207/S15326977EA0803_02

Al Otaiba, S., & Fuchs, D. (2002). Characteristics of children who are unresponsive to early literacy intervention: A review of the literature. *Remedial and Special Education, 23,* 300–316. http://dx.doi.org/10.1177/07419325020230050501

Alder, N. (2002). Interpretations of the meaning of care: Creating caring relationships in urban middle school classrooms. *Urban Education, 37*(2), 241-266. http://dx.doi.org/10.1177/0042085902372005

Amori, B., & Dalton, E. F. (1996). *Technical manual: IDEA oral language proficiency test Spanish (IPT I Oral Grades K-6;* 2nd ed.). Brea, CA: Ballard & Tighe.

Antunez, B. (2002). Implementing Reading First with English language learners. *Directions in Language & Education, 15,* 1–12.

Arce, J. (2000). Developing voices: Transformative education in a first grade two-way Spanish immersion classroom, a participatory study. *Bilingual Research Journal, 24,* 249–260.

Arias, B., & Morillo-Campbell, M. (2008). *Promoting ELL parental involvement: Challenges in contested times.* Tempe, AZ: Educational Policy Research Unit.

Artiles, A. J., Rueda, R., Salazar, J., & Higareda, I. (2005). Within-group diversity in minority disproportionate representation: ELLs in urban school districts. *Exceptional Children, 71,* 283–300.

Aud, S., Hussar, W., Kena, G., Bianco, K., Frohlich, L., Kemp, J., & Tahan, K. (2011). *The Condition of Education 2011* (NCES 2011-033). Washington, DC: U.S. Department of Education, National Center for Education Statistics.

August, D., & Hakuta, K. (Eds.). (1997). *Improving schooling for language-minority children: A research agenda.* Washington, DC: National Academy Press.

August, D., & Shanahan, T. (Eds.). (2006). *Developing literacy in second-language learners: A report of the National Literacy Panel on language-minority children and youth.* Mahwah, NJ: Erlbaum.

Avalos, M. A., Plasencia, A., Chavez, C., & Rascón, J. (2007). Modified guided reading: Gateway to English as a second language and literacy learning. *The Reading Teacher, 61,* 318-329. http://dx.doi.org/10.1598/RT.61.4.4

Baca, L., & Cervantes, H. (2004). *The bilingual special education interface.* Upper Saddle River, NJ: Pearson.

Baker, C. (2001). *Foundations of bilingual education and bilingualism* (3rd ed.). Clevedon, England: Multilingual Matters.

Baker, D. L., & Good, R. H. (2006). Fluidez en el relato oral. In D. L. Baker, R. H. Good, N. Knutson, & J. M. Watson (Eds.), *Indicadores dinámicos del éxito en la lectura* (7a ed.). Eugene, OR: Dynamic Measurement Group.

Barker, H. B., & Grassi, E. (2011). Culturally relevant practices for the special education eligibility process. *AccELLerate, 3*(3), 2–4.

Bender, W. (2002). *Differentiating instruction for students with learning disabilities: Best teaching practices for general and special educators.* Thousand Oaks, CA: Corwin Press.

Bhattacharjee, Y. (2012, March 17). The benefits of bilingualism. *The New York Times*, p. SR12. Retrieved from http://www.nytimes.com/2012/03/18/opinion/sunday/the-benefits-of-bilingualism.html

Bialystok, E. (2001). *Bilingualism in development: Language, literacy, & cognition.* New York, NY: Cambridge University Press.

Blue-Banning, M., Summers, J. A., Frankland, H. C., Nelson, L. L., & Beegle, G. (2004). Dimensions of family and professional partnerships: Constructive guidelines for collaboration. *Exceptional Children, 70*, 167–184.

Brenner, M. E. (1998). Adding cognition to the formula for culturally relevant instruction in mathematics. *Anthropology & Education Quarterly, 29*, 214–244. http://dx.doi.org/10.1525/aeq.1998.29.2.214

Bronfenbrenner, U. (1979). *The ecology of human development: Experiments by nature and design.* Cambridge, MA: Harvard University Press.

Brown, J. E., & Doolittle, J. (2008, May/June). A cultural, linguistic, and ecological framework for response to intervention with English language learners. *TEACHING Exceptional Children, 40*(5), 66–72.

Carrasquillo, A. L., & Rodriguez, J. (1997). Hispanic limited English proficient students with disabilities. *Learning Disabilities: A Multidisciplinary Journal, 8*, 167–174.

Cazden, C. B. (2001). *Classroom discourse: The language of teaching and learning* (2nd ed.). Portsmouth, NH: Heinemann.

Chalfant, J., & Pysh, M. (1989). Teacher assistance teams: Five descriptive studies on 96 teams. *Remedial and Special Education, 10*(6), 49–58. http://dx.doi.org/10.1177/074193258901000608

Chiappe, P., Siegel, L. S., & Gottardo, A. (2002). Reading-related skills of kindergartners from diverse linguistic backgrounds. *Applied Psycholinguistics Journal, 23(1)*, 95–116.

Cloud, N., Genesee, F., & Hamayan, E. (2009). *Literacy instruction for English language learners. A teacher's guide to research-based practices.* Portsmouth, NH: Heinemann.

Collier, C. (2005). Separating language difference from disability. *NABE News, 28*(3), 13–17.

Colorado Department of Education. (2009). *Response to intervention (RtI) family & community partnering: "On the team and at the table" toolkit.* Retrieved from http://www.cde.state.co.us/sites/default/files/documents/rti/downloads/pdf/familycommunitytoolkit.pdf

Crawford, J. (2004). *Educating English learners: Language diversity in the classroom* (5th ed.). Los Angeles, CA: Bilingual Education Services.

Crosson, A. C., & Lesaux, N. K. (2009). Revisiting assumptions about the relationship of fluent reading to comprehension: Spanish-speakers' text-reading fluency in English. *Reading and Writing: A Disciplinary Journal, 23,* 475–494. http://dx.doi.org/10.1007/s11145-009-9168-8

Cummins, J. (1979). Linguistic interdependence and the educational development of bilingual children. *Review of Educational Research, 49,* 221–251. http://dx.doi.org/10.3102/00346543049002222

Cummins, J. (1981). The role of primary language development in promoting educational success for language minority students. In *Schooling and language minority students: A theoretical framework* (1st ed., pp. 3-49). Sacramento, CA: California State Department of Education Office of Bilingual Bicultural Education.

Cummins, J. (1986). Empowering minority students: A framework for intervention. *Harvard Educational Review, 56,* 18–36.

Cummins, J. (1989). A theoretical framework for bilingual special education. *Exceptional Children, 56,* 111–119.

Cummins, J. (2000). *Language, power and pedagogy: Bilingual children in the crossfire.* Clevedon, England: Multilingual Matters.

De Ramirez, R., & Shapiro, E. (2006). Curriculum-based measurement and the evaluation of reading skills of Spanish-speaking English language learners in bilingual education classrooms. *School Psychology Review, 35,* 356–369.

Dixon, L. Q., Zhao, J., Shin, J. Y., Wu, S., Su, J. H., Burgess-Brigham, R., . . . Snow, C. (2012). What we know about second language acquisition: A synthesis from four perspectives. *Review of Educational Research, 82,* 5–60. http://dx.doi.org/10.3102/0034654311433587

Doherty, R. W., Echevarria, J., Estrada, P. E., Goldenberg, C., Hilberg, R. S., Saunders, W. M., & Tharp, R. G. (2002). *Research evidence: Five standards for effective pedagogy and student outcomes* (Technical Report No. G1). Santa Cruz, CA: University of California, CREDE.

Dunn, D. M., & Dunn, L. M. (2007). *Peabody picture vocabulary test, fourth edition, manual.* Minneapolis, MN: NCS Pearson.

Dunn, L.W., Padilla, Lugo, & Dunn, L. M. (1986). Test de vocabulario en imágenes Peabody. Circle Pines, MN: American Guidance Service.

Durgunoglu, A. Y., Nagy, W. E., & Hancin-Bhatt, B. J. (1993). Cross-language transfer of phonological awareness. *Journal of Educational Psychology, 85,* 453–465. http://dx.doi.org/10.1037/0022-0663.85.3.453

Durkin, D. (1979). What classroom observations reveal about reading comprehension instruction. *Reading Research Quarterly, 14,* 481–538. http://dx.doi.org/10.1598/RRQ.14.4.2

Ehri, L., Nunes, S., Willows, D., Schuster, B., Yaghoub-Zadeh, Z., & Shanahan, T. (2001). Phonemic awareness instruction helps children learn to read: Evidence from the National Reading Panel's meta-analysis. *Reading Research Quarterly, 36,* 250–287. http://dx.doi.org/10.1598/RRQ.36.3.2

Eppolito, A. (2011). *The response to intervention decision-making process for English language learners: Three elementary school case studies* (Doctoral dissertation). University of Colorado at Boulder. Retrieved from http://search.proquest.com/docview/915157719

Epstein, J., & Dauber, S. (1991). School programs and teacher practices of parent involvement in inner-city elementary and middle schools. *Elementary School Journal, 91,* 291–305. http://dx.doi.org/10.1086/461656

Epstein, J. L, Sanders, M. G., Simon, B. S., Salinas, K. C, Jansorn, N. R., & Van Voorhis, F. L. (2009). *School, family, and community partnerships: Your handbook for action.* Thousand Oaks, CA: Corwin Press.

Escamilla, K. (2000). Bilingual means two: Assessment issues, early literacy and Spanish-speaking children. *Reading Research Symposium for Second Language Learners* (pp. 1–16). Washington, DC: National Clearinghouse for Bilingual Education.

Escamilla, K., Geisler, D., Hopewell, S., Sparrow, W., & Butvilofsky, S. (2009). Using writing to make cross-language connections from Spanish to English. In C. Rodriguez (Ed.), *Achieving literacy success with English language learners* (pp. 141–156). Columbus, OH: Reading Recovery Council of North America.

Escamilla, K., Hopewell, S., Sparrow, W., & Butvilofsky, S., Escamilla, M., Soltero-Gonzalez, L. (2010). *Literacy squared.* www.literacysquared.org.

Esler, A. N., Godber, Y., & Christenson, S. L. (2008). Best practices in supporting school–family partnerships. In A. Thomas & J. Grimes (Eds.), *Best practices in school psychology V* (pp. 917–936). Bethesda, MD: NASP.

Ferris, D. R. (2002). *Treatment of error in second language student writing.* Ann Arbor, MI: The University of Michigan Press.

Figueroa, R., & Newsome, P. (2006). The diagnosis of LD in English learners. Is it non-discriminatory? *Journal of Learning Disabilities, 39,* 206–214. http://dx.doi.org/10.1177/00222194060390030201

Figueroa, R., & Sassenrath, J. (1989). A longitudinal study of the predictive validity of the system of multicultural pluralistic assessment (SOMPA). *Psychology in the Schools, 26,* 5–19. http://dx.doi.org/10.1002/1520-6807(198901)26:1<5::AID-PITS2310260102>3.0.CO;2-D

Fisher, D., & Frey, N. (2010). *Implementing RTI with English language learners.* Bloomington, IN: Solution Tree Press.

Francis, D. J., Rivera, M., Lesaux, N., Kieffer, M., & Rivera, H. (2006). *Practical guidelines for the education of English language learners: Research-based recommendations for instruction and academic interventions.* Houston, TX: Center on Instruction.

Freeman, Y., & Freeman, D. (2002). *Closing the achievement gap: How to reach limited-formal-schooling and long-term English language learners.* Portsmouth, NH: Heinemann.

Fry, R., & Lopez, M. H. (2012). *Hispanic student enrollment reach new highs in 2011.* Washington, DC: Pew Hispanic Center. Retrieved from http://www.pewhispanic.org/2012/08/20/hispanic-student-enrollments-reach-new-highs-in-2011/

Fuchs, D., Fuchs, L. S., & Bahr, M. W. (1990). Mainstream assistance teams: Scientific basis for the art of consultation. *Exceptional Children, 57,* 128–139.

Fuchs, D., Fuchs, L. S., & Burish, P. (2000). Peer-assisted learning strategies: An evidence-based practice to promote reading achievement. *Learning Disabilities Research and Practice, 15,* 85–91. http://dx.doi.org/10.1207/SLDRP1502_4

Fuchs, L., & Fuchs, D. (1997). Use of curriculum-based measurement in identifying students with disabilities. *Focus on Exceptional Children, 30,* 1–16.

Garcia, S., & Tyler, B. (2010). Meeting the needs of ELLs with LD in the general curriculum. *Theory Into Practice, 49,* 113–120. http://dx.doi.org/10.1080/00405841003626585

Gay, G. (2000). *Culturally responsive teaching: Theory, research, & practice.* New York, NY: Teachers College Press.

Gay, G. (2002). Preparing for culturally responsive teaching. *Journal of Teacher Education, 53,* 106-116. http://dx.doi.org/10.1177/0022487102053002003

Genesee, F., Geva, E., Dressler, C., & Kamil, M. (2006). In D. August & D. Shanahan (Eds), *Developing literacy in second-language learners* (pp. 153-174). Mahwah, NJ: Erlbaum and Washington, DC: Center for Applied Linguistics.

Genesee, F., Lindholm-Leary, K. J., Saunders, W., & Christian, D. (2006). *Educating English language learners.* New York, NY: Cambridge University Press.

Genesee, F., & Nicoladis, E. (2006). Bilingual first language acquisition. In E. Hoff & M. Shatz (Eds.), *Handbook of language development* (pp. 324–342). Oxford, England: Blackwell.

Genesee, F., & Riches, C. (2006). Literacy: Instructional issues. In F. Genesee, K. Lindholm-Leary, W. Saunders, & D. Christian (Eds.). *Educating English language learners: A synthesis of research evidence* (pp. 109–175). Cambridge, England: Cambridge University Press.

Gentile, L. (2004). What I have learned about reading and teaching children least experienced in language and literacy. *The California Reader, 38*(2), 31–38.

Gersten, R., & Baker, S. (2000). What we know about effective instructional practices for English-language learners. *Exceptional Children, 66,* 454–470.

Gersten, R., Baker, S. K., Collins, P., Linan-Thompson, S., Scarcella, R., & Shanahan, T. (2007). *Effective literacy and English language instruction for English learners in the elementary grades: A practice guide* (NCEE 2007-4011). Washington, DC: National Center for Education Evaluation and Regional Assistance. Retrieved from http://ies.ed.gov/ncee/wwc/publications/practiceguides

Gersten, R., Beckmann, S., Clarke, B., Foegen, A., Marsh, L., Star, J. R., & Witzel, B. (2009). *Assisting students struggling with mathematics: Response to intervention (RtI) for elementary and middle schools* (NCEE 2009-4060). Washington, DC: National Center for Education Evaluation and Regional Services, Institute of Education Sciences, U.S. Department of Education.

Gleitman, L., & Landau, B. (Eds.). (1994). *The acquisition of the lexicon.* Cambridge, MA: MIT Press.

Goldenberg, C. (2008, Summer). Teaching English language learners: What the research does—and does not—say. *American Educator, 32*(2), 8–23, 42–44.

Good, R. H., & Kaminski, R. A. (Eds.). (2002). *Dynamic indicators of basic early literacy skills* (6th ed.). Eugene, OR: Institute for the Development of Educational Achievement.

Grabe, W. (2009). *Reading in a second language: Moving from theory to practice.* New York, NY: Cambridge University Press.

Gravois, T. A., & Rosenfield, S. A. (2006). Impact of instructional consultation teams on the disproportionate referral and placement of minority students in special education. *Remedial and Special Education, 27,* 42–51. http://dx.doi.org/10.1177/07419325060270010501

Greene, J. (1997). A meta-analysis of the Rossell and Baker review of bilingual education research. *Bilingual Research Journal, 21,* 103–122. http://dx.doi.org/10.1080/15235882.1997.10668656

Grosjean, F., & Li, P. (2013). *The psycholinguistics of bilingualism.* Malden, MA: Wiley-Blackwell.

Haager, D., Klingner, J. K., & Aceves, T. (2009). *How to teach English language learners: Effective strategies from outstanding educators.* San Francisco, CA: Jossey Bass.

Hammer, C. S., Davison, M. D., Lawrence, F. R., & Miccio, A.W. (2009). The effect of home language on bilingual children's vocabulary and emergent literacy development during Head Start and kindergarten [Special issue]. *Scientific Studies of Reading, 13,* 99–121. http://dx.doi.org/10.1080/10888430902769541

Harper, C. A., & de Jong, E. J. (2004). Misconceptions about teaching ELLs. *Journal of Adolescent and Adult Literacy, 48,* 152–162. http://dx.doi.org/10.1598/JAAL.48.2.6

Harry, B., & Klingner, J. K. (2006). *Why are so many minority students in special education? Understanding race and disability in schools.* New York, NY: Teachers College Press.

Hemphill, F. C., & Vanneman, A. (2011, June). *Achievement gaps: How Hispanic and white students in public schools perform in mathematics and reading on the national assessment of educational progress. Statistical analysis report.* Washington, DC: U.S. Department of Education, National Center of Education Statistics. Retrieved from http://nces.ed.gov/nationsreportcard/pdf/studies/2011459.pdf

Herrera, S. G., Perez, D. R., & Escamilla, K. (2010). *Teaching reading to English language learners: Differentiated literacies.* Boston, MA: Allyn & Bacon.

Hiebert, E.H., Pearson, P.D., Taylor, B.M., Richardson, V., & Paris, S.G. (1998). *Every child a reader: Applying reading research in the classroom.* Ann Arbor: Center for the Improvement of Early Reading Achievement, University of Michigan School of Education.

Hoover, J. (2008). *Differentiating learning differences from disabilities: Meeting diverse needs through multi-tiered response to intervention.* Upper Saddle River, NJ: Pearson.

Hosp, J. L., & Reschly, D. J. (2003). Referral rates for intervention or assessment: A meta-analysis of racial differences. *The Journal of Special Education, 37,* 67–80. http://dx.doi.org/10.1177/00224669030370020201

Huerta, T. M. (2011). Humanizing pedagogy: Beliefs and practices on teaching of Latino children. *Bilingual Research Journal, 34*(1), 38-57. http://dx.doi.org/10.1080/15235882.2011.568826

Ikeda, M. J., Rahn-Bkadeskee, A., Niebling, B. C., Gustafson, J. K., Allison, R., & Stumme, J. (2007). The heartland area education agency 11 problem-solving approach: An overview and lessons learned. In S. R. Jimerson, M. K. Burns, & A. M. VanDerHeyden (Eds.). *Handbook of response to intervention: The science and practice of assessment and intervention* (pp. 255–268). New York, NY: Springer.

Individuals With Disabilities Education Act, 20 U.S.C. §§ 1400 *et seq.* (2006 & Supp. V.2011).

Kane, W. (2010, November 13). Latino kids now majority in state's public schools. *San Francisco Chronicle,* Retrieved from http://sfgate.com

Klingner, J., Almanza de Schonewise, E., de Onis, C., Méndez Barletta, L., & Hoover, J. (2008). Misconceptions about the second language acquisition process. In J. K. Klingner, J. Hoover, & L. Baca (Eds.), *English language learners who struggle with reading: Language acquisition or learning disabilities?* (pp. 17–35). Thousand Oaks, CA: Corwin Press.

Klingner, J. K., & Artiles, A. (2003). When should bilingual students be in special education? *Educational Leadership, 61*(2), 66–71.

Klingner, J. K., Artiles, A. J., & Méndez Barletta, L. (2006). English language learners who struggle with reading. Language acquisition or learning disabilities? *Journal of Learning Disabilities, 39,* 108–128.

Klingner, J., Boelé, A., Linan-Thompson, S., & Rodriguez, D. (2014). Essential components of special education for English language learners with learning disabilities. Position statement of the Division for Learning Disabilities of the Council for Exceptional Children. Arlington, VA: Council for Exceptional Children Division for Learning Disabilities. .

Klingner, J. K., & Edwards, P. A. (2006). Cultural considerations with response to intervention models. *Reading Research Quarterly, 41,* 108–117. http://dx.doi.org/10.1598/RRQ.41.1.6

Klingner, J. K., & Harry, B. (2006). The special education referral and decision-making process for English language learners: Child study team meetings and placement conferences. *Teachers College Record, 108,* 2247–2281. http://dx.doi.org/10.1111/j.1467-9620.2006.00781.x

Klingner, J. K., Hoover, J., & Baca, L. (2008). *Why do English Language Learners struggle with reading? Distinguishing language acquisition from learning disabilities.* Thousand Oaks, CA: Corwin Press.

Klingner, J. K., Soltero-González, L., & Lesaux, N. (2010). Response to intervention for English language learners. In M. Lipson & K. Wixson (Eds.), *Successful approaches to response to intervention (RTI): Collaborative practices for improving K–12 literacy* (pp. 134–162). Newark, DE: International Reading Association.

Klingner, J. K., & Vaughn, S. (1999). Promoting reading comprehension, content learning, and English acquisition through collaborative strategic reading (CSR). *The Reading Teacher, 52,* 738–747.

Klingner, J. K., & Vaughn, S. (2000). The helping behaviors of fifth-graders while using collaborative strategic reading (CSR) during ESL content classes. *TESOL Quarterly, 34,* 69–98. http://dx.doi.org/10.2307/3588097

Klingner, J. K., Vaughn, S., Argüelles, M. E., Hughes, M. T., & Ahwee, S. (2004). Collaborative strategic reading: "Real world" lessons from classroom teachers. *Remedial and Special Education, 25,* 291–302. http://dx.doi.org/10.1177/07419325040250050301

Klingner, J. K., Vaughn, S., & Boardman, A. (in press). *Teaching reading comprehension to students with learning difficulties* (2nd ed.). New York, NY: Guilford.

Klingner, J. K., Vaughn, S., Boardman, A., & Swanson, E. (2012). *Now we get it! Boosting comprehension with collaborative strategic reading.* San Francisco, CA: Jossey Bass.

Klingner, J. K., Vaughn, S., Schumm, J. S. (1998). Collaborative strategic reading during social studies in heterogeneous fourth-grade classrooms. *Elementary School Journal, 99,* 3–21. http://dx.doi.org/10.1086/461914

Kovaleski, J. F., & Pedersen, J. (2008). Best practices in data analysis teaming. In A. Thomas & J. Grimes (Eds.), *Best practices in school psychology V* (pp. 115–130). Bethesda, MD: National Association of School Psychologists.

Krashen, S. (1981). *Second language acquisition and second language learning.* Oxford, England: Pergamon Press.

Kress, J. (2008). *The ESL/ELL teachers' book of lists.* San Francisco, CA: Jossey-Bass.

Ladson-Billings, G. (1994). *The dreamkeepers: Successful teachers for African-American children.* San Francisco, CA: Jossey-Bass.

Ladson-Billings, G. (1995). Toward a theory of culturally relevant pedagogy *American Educational Research Journal, 32,* 465–491. http://dx.doi. org/10.3102/00028312032003465

Ladson-Billings, G. (2001). *Crossing over to Canaan: The journey of new teachers in diverse classrooms.* San Francisco, CA: Jossey-Bass.

Lesaux, N., & Marietta, S. (2012). *Making assessment matter: Using test results to differentiate reading instruction.* New York, NY: Guilford Press.

Lesaux, N., & Siegel, L. (2003). The development of reading in children who speak English as a second language. *Developmental Psychology, 39,* 1005–1019. http://dx.doi. org/10.1037/0012-1649.39.6.1005

Linan-Thompson, S., Bryant, D. P., Dickson, S. V., & Kouzekanani, K. (2005). Spanish literacy instruction for at-risk kindergarten students. *Remedial and Special Education, 26,* 236–244. http://dx.doi.org/10.1177/07419325050260040601

Linan-Thompson, S., Vaughn, S., Hickman-Davis, P. & Kouzekanani, K. (2003). Effectiveness of supplemental reading instruction for second-grade English language learners with reading difficulties. *The Elementary School Journal, 103,* 221–238. http://dx.doi. org/10.1086/499724

Linan-Thompson, S., Vaughn, S., Prater, K., & Cirino, P. (2006). The response to intervention of English language learners at risk for reading problems. *Journal of Learning Disabilities, 39,* 390–398. http://dx.doi.org/10.1177/00222194060390050201

Lindsey, K. A., Manis, F. R., & Bailey, C. E. (2003). Prediction of first-grade reading in Spanish-speaking English-language learners. *Journal of Educational Psychology, 95,* 482–494.

López-Reyna, N. (1996). The importance of meaningful contests in bilingual special education: Moving to whole language. *Learning Disabilities Research & Practice, 11,* 120–131.

Lucas, T., Villegas, A. M., & Freedson-Gonzalez, M. (2008). Linguistically responsive teacher education: Preparing classroom teachers to teach English language learners. *Journal of Teacher Education, 59,* 361–373. http://dx.doi.org/10.1177/0022487108322110

MacSwan, J. (2000). The threshold hypothesis, semilingualism, and other contributions to a deficit view of linguistic minorities. *Hispanic Journal of Behavioral Sciences, 22*(1), 3–45. http://dx.doi.org/10.1177/0739986300221001

MacSwan, J., & Rolstad, K. (2006). How language tests mislead us about children's abilities: Implications for special education placements. *Teachers College Record, 108,* 2304–2328. http://dx.doi.org/10.1111/j.1467-9620.2006.00783.x

MacSwan, J., Rolstad, K., & Glass, G. (2002). Do some school-age children have no language? Some problems of construct validity in the Pre-LAS Español. *Bilingual Research Journal, 26,* 395–420. http://dx.doi.org/10.1080/15235882.2002.10668718

Marple Newtown Sch. Dist. v. Raphael, 2007 WL 2458076 (E.D.Pa. 2007)

Martin-Rhee, M., & Bialystok, E. (2008). The development of two types of inhibitory control in monolingual and bilingual children. *Bilingualism: Language and Cognition 11*(1), 81–93. http://dx.doi.org/10.1017/S1366728907003227

Martinez, J. (2013). How do newcomer families adjust to school? *Cultural Connections: Eagle County School District Newsletter*. Eagle, CO: Eagle County School District.

Martinez, S. & Batsche, G. (2008) *Data-based decision-making: Academic and behavioral applications.* Retrieved from http://www.floridarti.usf.edu/resources/presentations/index.html

Mayer, M. (1969). *Frog, where are you?* New York, NY: Dial Press.

McLaughlin, B. (1992). *Myths and misconceptions about second language learning: What every teacher needs to unlearn.* Santa Cruz, CA: National Center for Research in Cultural Diversity and Second Language Learning.

Menken, K., & Kleyn T. (April 2009). The difficult road for long-term English learners. *Educational Leadership, 66*(7). Retrieved from http://www.ascd.org/publications/educational_leadership/apr09/vol66/num07/The_Difficult_Road_for_Long-Term_English_Learners.aspx

Moll, L. C., Amanti, C., Neff, D., & Gonzalez, N. (1992). Funds of knowledge for teaching: Using a qualitative approach to connect homes and classrooms. *Theory Into Practice, 31,* 132–141. http://dx.doi.org/10.1080/00405849209543534

Moll, L. C., & Greenberg, J. (1990). Creating zones of possibilities: Combining social contexts for instruction. In L.C. Moll (Ed.), *Vygotsky and education* (pp. 319–348). Cambridge, England: Cambridge University Press.

Moore-Brown, B., Huerta, M., Uranga-Hernandez, Y., Pena, E. (2006). Using dynamic assessment to evaluate children with suspected learning disabilities. *Intervention in School and Clinic, 41,* 209–217. http://dx.doi.org/10.1177/10534512060410040301

Moses Guccione, L. (2012). *Oral language development and ELLs: 5 challenges and solutions.* Retrieved from http://www.colorincolorado.org/article/50910/

National Center for Education Statistics. (2009). Table A-6-1. Number and percentage distribution of 3- to 21-year olds served under the Individuals with Disabilities Education Act (IDEA), Part B, and number served as a percentage of total public school enrollment, by type of disability: Selected school years, 1976–77 through 2007–08.Washington, DC: Institute of Education Sciences, U.S. Department of Education. Retrieved from http://nces.ed.gov/programs/coe/2010/section1/table-cwd-1.asp

National Clearinghouse for English Language Acquisition. (2011, February). *The growing numbers of English learner students, 1998/99-2008/09.* Retrieved from http://www.ncela.us/files/uploads/9/growingLEP_0809.pdf

Nelson, J. R, Benner, G. J., & Gonzalez, J. (2003). Learner characteristics that influence the treatment effectiveness of early literacy interventions: A meta analytic review. *Learning Disabilities Research & Practice, 18,* 255–267. http://dx.doi.org/10.1111/1540-5826.00080

Nessel, D., & Dixon, C. (2008). *Using the language experience approach with English language learners: Strategies for engaging students and developing literacy.* Thousand Oaks, CA: Sage.

Nieto, S. (2003). *What keeps teachers going?* New York, NY: Teachers College Press.

Nieto, S. (2004). *Affirming diversity: The sociopolitical context of multicultural education* (4th ed.). Boston, MA: Pearson Education.

O'Connor, R., Bocian, K., Beebe-Frankenberger, M., & Linklater, D. (2010). Responsiveness of students with language difficulties to early intervention in reading. *The Journal of Special Education, 43,* 220–235. http://dx.doi.org/10.1177/0022466908317789

O'Connor, R., & Klingner, J. (2010). Poor responders in RTI. *Theory Into Practice, 49* 297–304. http://dx.doi.org/10.1080/00405841.2010.510758

Orosco, M. (2010). A sociocultural examination of response to intervention with Latino English language learners. *Theory Into Practice, 49,* 265–272. http://dx.doi.org/10.1080/00405841.2010.510703

Orosco, M., & Klingner, J. K. (2010). One school's implementation of RTI with English language learners: "Referring into RTI." *Journal of Learning Disabilities, 43,* 269–288. http://dx.doi.org/10.1177/0022219409355474

Ovando, O., Collier, V., & Combs, M. (2003). *Bilingual and ESL classrooms: Teaching in multicultural contexts.* Boston, MA: McGraw Hill.

Peña, E. E., Bedore, L. M., & Gillam, R. B. (2011). Two to untangle: Language impairment and language differences in bilinguals. *AccELLerate, 3*(3), 7–9.

Peregoy, S. F., & Boyle, O. F. (2008). *Reading, writing, and learning in ESL: A resource book for K–12 teachers* (5th ed.). New York, NY: Addison-Wesley.

Petrovic, J. E. (Ed.). (2010). *International perspectives on bilingual education: Policy, practice, and controversy.* Charlotte, NC: Information Age Publishing.

Pinker, S. (1994). *The language instinct.* New York, NY: Morrow.

Portes, A., & Rumbaut, R. G. (2001). *Legacies: The story of the immigrant second generation.* Berkeley, CA: University of California Press.

Pugach, M. C., & Johnson, L. J. (1995). Unlocking expertise among classroom teachers through structured dialogue: Extending research on peer collaboration. *Exceptional Children, 62,* 101–110.

Rolstad, K., Mahoney, K., & Glass, G. (2005). The big picture: A meta-analysis of program effectiveness research on English Language Learners. *Educational Policy, 19,* 572–594. http://dx.doi.org/10.1177/0895904805278067

Reyes, I., & Azuara, P. (2008). Emergent biliteracy in young Mexican immigrant children. *Reading Research Quarterly, 43* (4) 374-398.

Rueda, R., MacGillivray, L., Monzó, L., & Arzubiaga, A. (2001). Engaged reading: A multi-level approach to considering sociocultural factors with diverse learners. In D. McInerny & S. VanEtten (Eds.), *Research on sociocultural influences on motivation and learning.* (pp. 233–264). Charlotte, NC: Information Age Publishing.

Saenz, L. M., Fuchs, L. S., & Fuchs, D. (2005). Peer-assisted learning strategies for English language learners with learning disabilities. *Exceptional Children, 71,* 231–247.

Samway, K., & McKeon, D. (2007). *Myths and realities: Best practices for English language learners* (2nd ed.). Portsmouth, NH: Heinemann.

Schwierjohn, C. A. (2011). *Identifying key factors in implementing and sustaining response to intervention: A comparison of schools currently implementing RTI* (Doctoral dissertation). Lindenwood University, St. Charles, MN.

Service, E., Simola, M., Metsanheimo, O., & Maury, S. (2002). Bilingual working memory span is affected by language skill. *European Journal of Cognitive Psychology, 14,* 383-407. doi: 10.1080/09541440143000140

Shinn, M. M., & Shinn, M. R. (2003). *Administration and scoring of early literacy measures for use with AIMSweb.* Eden Prairie, MN: Edformation.

Short, D. J., & Fitzsimmons, S. (2007). *Double the work: Challenges and solutions to acquiring language and academic literacy for adolescent English language learners.* Washington, DC: Alliance for Excellent Education.

Slavin, R. E., & Cheung, A. (2005). A synthesis of research on language of reading instruction for English language learners. *Review of Educational Research, 75,* 247–284. http://dx.doi.org/10.3102/00346543075002247

Smith, M. (2012, August 31). At some schools, the demographics future is now. *The New York Times.* Retrieved from http://www.nytimes.com

Snow, C. E., Burns, M. S., & Griffin, P. (Eds.). (1998). *Preventing reading difficulties in young children.* Washington, DC: National Academy Press.

Snow, C. E., Lawrence, J. F., & White, C. (2009). Generating knowledge of academic language among urban middle school students. *Journal of Research on Educational Effectiveness, 2,* 325–344. http://dx.doi.org/10.1080/19345740903167042

Spinelli, C. G. (2008). Addressing the issue of cultural and linguistic diversity and assessment: Informal evaluation measures for English language learners. *Reading & Writing Quarterly, 24,* 101–118.

Stahl, S. A., & Murray, B. A. (1994). Defining phonological awareness and its relationship to early reading. *Journal of Educational Psychology, 86,* 221–234. http://dx.doi.org/10.1037//0022-0663.86.2.221

Sullivan, A. (2011). Disproportionality in special education identification and placement of ELLs. *Exceptional Children, 71,* 317–334.

Tager-Flusberg, H. (1997). Language acquisition and theory of mind: Contributions from the study of autism. In L.B. Adamson & M.A. Romski (Eds.), *Research on communication and language disorders: Contributions to theories of language development* (pp. 133–158). Baltimore, MD: Brookes.

Takakuwa, M. (2003, April-May). *Lessons from a paradoxical hypothesis: A methodological critique of the threshold hypothesis.* ElPadás: 4th International Symposium on Bilingualism. Arizona State University, Phoenix.

Teachers of English to Speakers of Other Languages. (2008). *TESOL/NCATE Standards for the recognition of initial programs in P-12 ESL teacher education.* Alexandria, VA: Author. Retrieved from http://www.tesol.org/s_tesol/sec_document.asp?CID=219&DID=10698

Thomas, W. P., & Collier, V. P. (2002). *A national study of school effectiveness for language minority students' long-term academic achievement.* Santa Cruz, CA: Center for Research on Education, Diversity and Excellence.

U.S. Department of Education. (2010, March). *A blueprint for reform. The reauthorization of the Elementary and Secondary Education Act.* Washington, DC: Author. Retrieved from http://www2.ed.gov/policy/elsec/leg/blueprint/blueprint.pdf

Valdés, G. (1996). *Con respeto: Bridging the distances between culturally diverse families and schools.* New York, NY: Teachers College Press.

Valdés, G. (2001). *Learning and not learning English: Latino students in American schools.* New York, NY: Teachers College Press.

Valdés, G., & Figueroa, R. A. (1994). *Bilingualism and testing: A special case of bias.* Norwood, NJ: Ablex.

VanDerHeyden, A., Witt, J., Gilbertson, D. (2007). A multi-year evaluation of the effects of a Response to Intervention (RTI) model on identification of children for special education. *Journal of School Psychology, 45,* 225–256. http://dx.doi.org/10.1016/j.jsp.2006.11.004

Vaughn, S., Cirino, P. T., Linan-Thompson, S., Mathes, P. G., Carlson, C. D., Hagan, E. C., . . . Francis, D. J. (2006). Effectiveness of a Spanish intervention and an English intervention for English language learners at risk for reading problems. *American Educational Research Journal, 43,* 449–487. http://dx.doi.org/10.3102/00028312043003449

Vaughn, S., Klingner, J. K., Swanson, E. A., Boardman, A. G., Roberts, G., Mohammed, S. S., & Stillman-Spisak, S. J. (2011). Efficacy of collaborative strategic reading with middle school students. *American Educational Research Journal, 48,* 938–964. http://dx.doi.org/10.3102/0002831211410305

Vaughn, S., Linan-Thompson, S., Mathes, P., Cirino, P., Carlson, C., Pollard- Durodola, S. D., . . . Francis, D. (2006a). First-grade English language learners at risk for reading problems: Effectiveness of an English intervention. *Elementary School Journal, 107,* 153–181. http://dx.doi.org/10.1086/510653

Vaughn, S., Linan-Thompson, S., Mathes, P. G., Cirino, P., Carlson, C. D., Pollard-Durodola, S.D., . . . Francis, D. (2006b). Effectiveness of a Spanish intervention and an English intervention for first-grade English language learners at risk for reading difficulties. *Journal of Learning Disabilities, 39,* 56–73. http://dx.doi.org/10.1177/00222194060390010601

Vaughn, S., Mathes, P., Linan-Thompson, S., & Francis, D. J. (2005). Teaching English language learners at risk for reading disabilities to read: Putting research into practice. *Learning Disabilities Research & Practice, 20,* 58–67. http://dx.doi.org/10.1111/j.1540-5826.2005.00121.x

Villegas, A. M., & Lucas, T. (2002). *Educating culturally responsive teachers: A coherent approach.* Albany, NY: SUNY Press.

Wechsler, D. (1991). *The Wechsler intelligence scale for children—Third edition.* San Antonio, TX: The Psychological Corporation.

Wilkinson, C. Y., Ortiz, A., Robertson, P. M., & Kushner, M. I. (2006). English language learners with reading-related LD: Linking data from multiple sources to make eligibility determinations. *Journal of Learning Disabilities, 39,* 129–141. http://dx.doi.org/10.1177/00222194060390020201

Wong Fillmore, L. (2000). Loss of family languages: Should educators be concerned? *Theory Into Practice, 39,* 203–210. http://dx.doi.org/10.1207/s15430421tip3904_3

Woodcock, R. W., & Muñoz-Sandoval, A. F. (1993). *Woodcock-Muñoz language survey comprehensive manual.* Chicago, IL: Riverside.

Ysseldyke, J. E. (2005). Assessment and decision making for students with learning disabilities: What if this is as good as it gets? *Learning Disability Quarterly, 28,* 125–128. http://dx.doi.org/10.2307/1593610

Zehler, A., Fleischman, H., Hopstock, P., Stephenson, T., Pendzick, M., & Sapru, S. (2003). *Policy report: Summary of findings related to LEP and SPED-LEP students.* Washington, DC: U.S. Department of Education Office. Retrieved from http://onlineresources.wnylc.net/pb/orcdocs/LARC_Resources/LEPTopics/ED/DescriptiveStudyofServicestoLEPStudentsandLEPStudentswithDisabilities.pdf